CITYSPOTS
GENEVA

WHAT'S IN YOUR GUIDEBOOK?

Independent authors Impartial up-to-date information from our travel experts who meticulously source local knowledge.

Experience Thomas Cook's 165 years in the travel industry and guidebook publishing enriches every word with expertise you can trust.

Travel know-how Contributions by thousands of staff around the globe, each one living and breathing travel.

Editors Travel-publishing professionals, pulling everything together to craft a perfect blend of words, pictures, maps and design.

You, the traveller We deliver a practical, no-nonsense approach to information, geared to how you really use it.

CITYSPOTS

GENEVA

Kerry Walker

Thomas Cook

Written by Kerry Walker
Original photography by Jonathan Smith
Front cover photography (Red Cross Museum) © Getty Images
Series design based on an original concept by Studio 183 Limited

Produced by Cambridge Publishing Management Limited
Project Editor: Penny Isaac
Layout: Paul Queripel
Maps: PC Graphics
Transport map: © Communicarta Limited

Published by Thomas Cook Publishing
A division of Thomas Cook Tour Operations Limited
Company Registration No. 1450464 England
PO Box 227, Unit 18, Coningsby Road
Peterborough PE3 8SB, United Kingdom
email: books@thomascook.com
www.thomascookpublishing.com
+ 44 (0) 1733 416477

ISBN: 978-1-84157-772-2

First edition © 2007 Thomas Cook Publishing
Text © 2007 Thomas Cook Publishing
Maps © 2007 Thomas Cook Publishing
Series/Project Editor: Kelly Anne Pipes
Production/DTP: Steven Collins

Printed and bound in Spain by GraphyCems

CONTENTS

CITYSPOTS

SYMBOLS KEY

The following symbols are used throughout this book:

ⓐ address ⓣ telephone ⓦ website address ⓔ email
ⓛ opening times Ⓝ public transport connections

The following symbols are used on the maps:

𝒊 information office	O	city
✈ airport	O	large town
✚ hospital	○	small town
🛡 police station	═	motorway
🚍 bus station	—	main road
🚆 railway station		minor road
✝ cathedral	—	railway
❶ numbers denote featured cafés & restaurants		

Hotels and restaurants are graded by approximate price
as follows:
£ budget ££ mid-range £££ expensive

▶ *Geneva's giant Floral Clock*

Introduction

Geneva is like a huge Swiss chocolate box, where each experience should be savoured: from the hum of life in the medieval Old Town to the pin-drop peace of the lakefront, where the early morning mist peels back to reveal Mont Blanc. On the surface this city is silky smooth, with its 5-star hotels, plush boutiques and gourmet haunts – but appearances can be deceptive. Bite beneath the surface and you'll get an explosion of different experiences.

Most surprising, perhaps, is the proximity of nature to the city, and the variation of its forms. Within spitting distance of the mighty UN headquarters, you can take a ride across Europe's largest alpine lake, its contours carved out by glaciers, sip home-grown Pinot Noirs in vine-clad Satigny, spot pink flamingos in the Jardin Botanique and whoosh down the French Alps on a pair of skis. And with promenades hugging the water's edge, this is one place you won't want to be without your walking boots.

This city of 180,000 inhabitants may be small, but it thinks big. The Cathédrale St Pierre towers above the cobbled Old Town, the 140-m (460-ft) Jet d'Eau fountain creates a rainbow with its spray and the enormous Horloge Fleurie (Floral Clock) raises eyebrows in the Jardin Anglais. If you want to indulge in culture, you can take your pick: from contemporary masterpieces at MAMCO, Monet at the Musée d'Art et d'Histoire and opera highs at the Grand Théâtre.

South of the centre, Carouge steals the Little Italy award with its low-slung Piedmont skyline, shady squares and kooky boutiques. A trip to the Left Bank brings you to the boho cafés and funky bars in Plainpalais, while on the Right is Pâquis – a knot of narrow streets where restaurants whip up world flavours and the hip crowd hangs out on the pier. Like all good chocolate boxes, Geneva really does offer something for everyone.

● *Statuesque beauty in Mon Repos park*

When to go

SEASONS & CLIMATE

Geneva has a temperate climate, but the northerly *bise* wind that blows down from the Alps can make it feel chilly, particularly around the lake. Mild springs spell fewer crowds and beautiful blooms in the city's gardens. Summers are warm but not too hot, peaking at around 25°C (77°F) – the time to see roses bloom in the Jardin Anglais, catch open-air music festivals and chill out on the Left Bank's beach.

In autumn, expect a final burst of colour in Geneva's parks and the odd shower; it is the ideal time to explore the city's galleries and enjoy leisurely strolls. Winters occasionally bring light snow, with temperatures hovering between 5°C (41°F) and a frosty –2°C (28.4°F). 'Tis the season to wrap up and head for the Christmas market and Place du Rhône's ice rink.

ANNUAL EVENTS

March

Geneva Carnival Costumed parades, streams of colourful floats, music, dancing, parties and street entertainment bring carnival fever to Geneva for three days in March. ❶ 079 382 92 77 ⓦ www.carnaval-geneve.ch

International Motor Show The city steps up a gear in spring when the motor-mad check out the latest in cars, technology and accessories at this mammoth exhibition held at the Palexpo. ⓐ Palexpo Exhibition Centre ❶ 022 761 11 11 ⓦ www.salon-auto.ch

April
AMR Jazz Festival Jazz, soul and blues rhythms at the Alhambra draw music lovers to Geneva in droves. ⓐ Alhambra ⓣ 022 716 56 30 ⓦ www.amr-geneve.ch

May
Geneva Marathon Thousands of runners cover a scenic route through the city. ⓐ Place des Nations ⓣ 022 304 07 72 ⓦ www.genevemarathon.ch

June
Fête de la Musique Streets and squares are transformed into open-air stages for this monster music festival, staging

◓ *Autumnal hues in Parc des Bastions*

everything from chanson to jazz and pop concerts.
☎ 022 418 65 00 Ⓦ www.fetedelamusique.ch

July–August
Musiques en Été From classical concerts to funky jazz, sopranos to African beats, this two-month festival breathes musical life into the city. ☎ 022 418 36 18 Ⓦ www.ville-ge.ch

Orange Cinema Catch the latest flicks on a giant, open-air screen at this summer film festival by the lake.
Ⓦ www.orangecinema.ch

August
Fêtes de Genève Parades, fireworks and late-night parties make this festival a highlight in Geneva's summer calendar. Best of all, it's free! ☎ 022 716 56 30 Ⓦ www.fetes-de-geneve.ch

September
Art'Air Artists seek inspiration in all corners of the city for this weekend of open-air workshops. ☎ 022 794 89 80
Ⓦ www.artair.ch Ⓔ info@artair.ch

La Bâtie Festival A celebration of dance, theatre and music across the city. ☎ 022 738 19 19 Ⓦ www.batie.ch

Fête des Vendanges Taste the produce of the grape harvest in the nearby village of Russin. As well as free-flowing wine, this intoxicating festival features markets, music and street entertainment. Ⓦ www.russin.ch

November–December
Christmas Market The twinkling market on Place de la Fusterie has stalls with handmade crafts, gingerbread and mulled wine. **ⓐ** Place de la Fusterie **ⓣ** 022 909 70 70 (tourist office)

November–January
Christmas Ice Rink Warm up with mulled wine and raclette after a stint on the ice. **ⓐ** Place du Rhône **ⓣ** 022 909 70 70 (tourist office)

December
Coup de Noël A teeth-chattering 125-m (410-ft) swim in Lake Geneva. **ⓐ** Jardin Anglais **ⓣ** 022 909 70 70 (tourist office)

Fête de l'Escalade History is revisited at this must-see event celebrating the city's victory in 1602 in riotous fashion. **ⓣ** 079 382 92 77 **ⓦ** www.compagniede1602.ch

> **PUBLIC HOLIDAYS**
> These dates show the official public holidays in Geneva:
> **New Year's Day** 1 January
> **Good Friday** Friday before Easter Sunday
> **Easter Monday** Day after Easter Sunday
> **Ascension Day** 40 days after Easter Sunday
> **Whit Monday** May/June (day after Pentecost)
> **Swiss National Day** 1 August
> **Geneva Fast** 7 September
> **Christmas Day** 25 December
> **Restauration Genèvoise** 31 December

Escalade

Fanfare parades, festive revelry and a whole lot of Swiss chocolate smashing make the Escalade the most important event of the year. Held on the weekend closest to 11 December, the unique celebrations commemorate the city's 1602 victory over the Duke of Savoy's troops, who tried to attack Geneva by scaling the city's walls at night. Genevan Catherine Cheynel, better known as the Mère Royaume, stopped some of the attackers dead in their tracks by pouring a pot of scalding vegetable soup over their heads – her determined resistance helped secure Geneva's independence.

The week before the big event kicks off with a race called the Course de L'Escalade, where hundreds of sprightly locals turn out to stampede through the Old Town's narrow streets to Parc des Bastions – a fun way to keep fit and take in the sights. Many of the runners wear flamboyant costumes.

On the following weekend, festivities build up to Sunday's torchlit parade; this marks the historical event with re-enactments complete with 17th-century costume and artillery demonstrations. As darkness falls, drummers, pipers and trumpeters march past, musketeers on horseback open fire and brave swordsmen display their skills. The noise is ear splitting and the atmosphere electric. The parade winds through the cobbled Old Town to Cathédrale St Pierre, where visitors can warm up with mugs of the infamous vegetable soup and spicy *vin chaud* (mulled wine).

The event culminates with the ritual smashing of the *marmite* (cooking pot). The difference is that today's pots are made of chocolate and filled with marzipan vegetables. The shelves of every *pâtisserie* and *confiserie* in Geneva stock these traditional treats, which should be shattered with a single blow (preferably not over someone's head): a sweet end to an ill-fated invasion.

○ *Marzipan vegetables commemorate an ancient victory*

History

Geneva has seen its fair share of incomers throughout its long and turbulent history, stretching back to 3000 BC when Celtic tribes first settled on the banks of Lake Geneva. The Romans conquered the town in 120 BC and the first written mention of 'Genua' was by Julius Caesar around 52 BC.

The year AD 350 marked a turning point in Geneva's history as Germanic Burgundians occupied the town and bishops took power there, making it their first capital in 443. Less than a century later, Franks stepped in and Geneva became part of the Merovingian Kingdom. In the 9th century, the Burgundian Kingdom retook the reins of power until 1032, when the last King of Burgundy died, at which point the German Empire took over.

Geneva blossomed in the Middle Ages and made its mark on the map with the growing importance of its trade fairs, underpinned by the *combourgeoisie*, an alliance which strengthened the bonds between Geneva, Bern and Fribourg. The Protestant Reformation played a pivotal role in shaping the city and was finally accepted by the people in 1536. Just three years later, one of the key figures in the movement, Jean Calvin, founded the city's college and academy.

At the beginning of the 17th century, attention turned to Savoy, which had for some time posed a threat to Geneva's independence. On the night of 11 December 1602, the Duke of Savoy's troops attempted once again to attack the city by climbing its walls using ladders. But they were driven away by the inhabitants, including the Mère Royaume, who threw a pot of piping hot vegetable soup over attacking soldiers. This is the event that is celebrated at the Escalade (see pages 14–15).

The 18th century spelt a golden age for Geneva, as the watch-making industry and banking sector flourished. Among the city's inhabitants at this time was famous writer and philosopher Jean-Jacques Rousseau, whose writings, proclaiming universal liberty and equality, sowed the seeds of the French Revolution. In 1798, Geneva was annexed to France, but regained its freedom in 1813 after the defeat of Napoleon.

A year after Henry Dunant established the Red Cross in 1863, the Geneva Convention was signed, calling for the protection of victims of war and conflict. These milestones laid the foundations for humanitarian law and explain why Geneva was chosen as the headquarters of the League of Nations in 1919. After World War II, Geneva became established as the European headquarters of the United Nations and boomed economically and socially. Today, Geneva continues to play a fundamental role in world affairs, with its ever-growing crop of international organisations, a prosperous service sector and a high standard of living.

⬥ *The Reformation Wall: figures who shaped the city*

Lifestyle

Life and style: Geneva has both in abundance, so it's no coincidence that this Swiss city ranked second in the Worldwide Quality of Living Survey 2006 (just behind big brother Zurich). A glance around reveals a clean, safe city with an excellent infrastructure, booming business and a superb range of chic restaurants and bars in which the hard-working residents love to play. You'll instantly feel at home in this welcoming,

● *Markets are part of Geneva's appealing mix*

cosmopolitan city, which is posh but not pretentious, attractive but not overblown, efficient but by no means dull.

The first thing that strikes you is Geneva's relaxed pace of life. With cheery locals that are happy to converse and cars that stop to let you cross the road, this feels a million miles away from the hustle and bustle of most metropolises. This laid-back atmosphere is undoubtedly influenced by the lake, the city's natural escape valve, which is surrounded by beautiful parks and dramatic mountain panoramas. Despite their Rolex watches and passion for champagne, Genevans are well-groomed country kids at heart. With the Alps on their doorstep for skiing in winter and beaches for swimming in summer, it's no wonder they go to work with a spring in their step.

With its mixture of languages and cultures, Geneva is a multi-ethnic melting pot. Genevans tend to have an open-minded attitude and liberal streak. Here, businessmen in smart suits share coffee with penniless poets, while Rastafarians and Portuguese bakers hang out with politicians at the Bains des Pâquis. Beneath the Swiss upper crust lies the world in miniature. Adding a dash of energy to the mix is the lively student population that accounts for the plethora of trendy cafés, ever-evolving art scene and late-night partying in high doses.

The good life is what most people associate with Switzerland and it's certainly true of Geneva, a city that epitomises *joie de vivre*. While locals work hard, they are also experts at enjoying themselves, which is why this grown-up playground is dedicated to every possible pastime – from casinos to wining, shopping to alfresco dining. So relax and savour this extraordinary city.

Culture

In many senses, Geneva is the cultural heart of Switzerland. No fewer than 30 world-class museums, as well as scores of galleries, theatres, concert halls and live music venues have established this city's international reputation for the arts. And culture here is as much about the present as the past: alive and everywhere. Whenever you visit, there's bound to be something raising the cultural barometer, whether on the stage, screen or canvas, from soulful rhythms at the AMR Jazz Festival to fancy footwork at La Bâtie Festival.

It doesn't matter where you go in Geneva: you can't escape music. If you're seeking classical highs, it has to be Place Neuve, home to the Grand Théâtre (the spitting image of Opéra Garnier in Paris), where the acclaimed Orchestre de la Suisse Romande performs, and the rococo-style Victoria Hall where strings and sopranos raise the roof. At the top of the alternative music tree,

ART OF THE ORDINARY

Causing a ripple of excitement in the Swiss art world, Geneva-born artist John M Armleder frequently displays his unique and intriguing work at MAMCO. Art in the ordinary is what his exhibitions are about, bringing together abstract paintings, sculpture, drawings and photos to depict the beauty of the banal. A prime example is furniture art, where tables and chairs are splashed with colour, suggesting that we're not only inspired by art, but also what surrounds it.

◆ *Absorbing culture at the Musée d'Art et d'Histoire*

innovative venues such as L'Usine, Salle Centrale and Le Chat Noir regularly host jam sessions and concerts from live jazz to world music, techno and rock.

Geneva has more than its fair share of excellent galleries that will satisfy the cravings of art buffs. At the top of the list is the Musée d'Art et d'Histoire, showcasing everything from prehistoric artefacts to masterpieces by Rodin and Konrad Witz. Housed in a former factory, MAMCO is its contemporary contender with its attention-grabbing temporary exhibitions. Other art gems include the Musée Ariana , which covers the entire spectrum of ceramics and glassware, and the Musée Rath, housing an exceptional fine-arts collection. Those that prefer their art outdoors should check out the wacky Schtroumpfs building on the Right Bank, with irregular lines, vivid colours and mosaic patterns that would give Gaudí a run for his money.

The stage has its part to play in Geneva's cultural life, too, with everything from classic to avant-garde productions. For high-quality ballet, opera and theatrical performances, book tickets for the Grand Théâtre or catch cutting-edge drama at the Comédie de Genève. The Théâtre du Grütli is a sound choice for improvised and quirky plays, while Théâtre de Carouge hosts a mix of experimental productions and timeless favourites. L'Usine is the city's darling of the daring and features an adventurous line-up and performances that always cross the boundaries of convention.

The spires of Cathédrale St Pierre

Shopping

Geneva makes no secret of its love for the finer things in life: markets piled high with the freshest produce, *chocolatiers* making mouths water with Swiss truffles and fashion designers showing off the latest trends.

Geneva's shops are open year-round, six days a week. Shopping hours are generally 09.00–19.00 Monday to Saturday, with smaller boutiques often closing for lunch. Major shopping malls and department stores stay open for late-night shopping until 21.00 on Thursdays.

SHOPPING STREETS

Sniff out the latest styles in the boutiques and high-street stores that pepper the Left Bank. For luxury brands, head for the diamond-encrusted Rue du Rhône and Rue de la Confédération, where glitzy creations in jewellers like Cartier and Bulgari come with a matching price tag. Carouge is the place to buy one-off crafts, from hand-thrown pots to pralines.

MALLS & DEPARTMENT STORES

Conveniently located near the station, Metro Shopping Cornavin is lined with high-street names like Swarovski, Lacoste and Yves Rocher. Nearby, the six-level Manor department store is the ideal one-stop shop, tempting shoppers to spend on fashion, fragrances and home design. Go to the top floor for panoramic views over Geneva. Slightly more upmarket, Globus on Rue du Rhône is well stocked with everything from funky footwear to gourmet flavours in the basement food court.

⬤ *Satisfy your shopping cravings*

MARKETS

Stalls brim with local produce such as fruit, flowers, cheese, honey and handmade breads every Wednesday and Saturday at Carouge's food market (08.00–13.00). While you're roaming the square, pause to taste freshly baked pastries, drink local wines and soak up the relaxed village atmosphere. On the same days, antique enthusiasts hunt for gems at the Plainpalais Flea Market (06.30–18.00), crammed with bric-à-brac, musty books, vintage clothes and old vinyl.

BEST BUYS

Multipurpose, classic red Victorinox army knives always make a useful gift. For a lingering taste of Geneva, buy a gift-wrapped box of Zeller's divine truffles or Philippe Pascoët's basil-infused pralines (if they last till you get home...). It wouldn't be Switzerland without Swatch – pick up arty watches at the store on Rue du Mont-Blanc.

USEFUL SHOPPING PHRASES

How much is this?
C'est combien?
Cey combyahng?

I'll take this one, thank you
Je prends celui-ci/
celle-ci, merci
*Zher prahng serlweesi/
sehlsee, mehrsee*

My size is...
Ma taille (clothes)/
ma pointure (shoes) est ...
*Mah tie/mah
pooahngtewr ay ...*

Can I try this on?
Puis-je essayer ceci?
Pweezh ehssayeh cerssee?

Eating & drinking

Geneva excels in the gastro department with hearty fare like cheese fondue and rösti on the menu. Dining here doesn't have to be expensive: virtually every restaurant has a good-value *plat du jour* that caters for the budget conscious. So whether you want to reach for the Michelin stars on the Quai du Mont-Blanc, eat your way around the world in Pâquis, or snuggle up in a wood-panelled bistro, this city has the place for you.

DINING DISTRICTS

Big on character and Swiss staples, the cobbled streets of the Old Town are stacked with cosy brasseries and alpine-style chalets serving dishes such as entrecôte steak and fondue. Many offer good-value lunch specials. Go underground to vaulted cellars where candles flicker, or pull up a chair on the terrace of a *petit bistro* on the Place du Bourg de Four for alfresco dining in summer.

For those with a bigger bank balance, the swish restaurants lining the glitzy Quai du Mont-Blanc and Quai Wilson beckon. This is the place to enjoy haute cuisine, 5-star service and prime views of Lake Geneva. Departing every Thursday and Friday,

PRICE RATING
The restaurant price guides used in this book indicate the approximate cost of a three-course meal for one person, excluding drinks, at the time of writing.
£ under CHF50   ££ CHF50–100   £££ over CHF100

fondue cruises offer a more affordable slice of luxury on the lake. ⓦ www.cgn.ch

Tired of cheese and chocolate? Head for Pâquis to savour world flavours. This hip corner of Geneva spices things up with everything from feisty Mexican enchiladas to hole-in-the-wall Moroccan oases. This multicultural district serves up everything from Lebanese to Thai, Japanese and Portuguese specialities.

Low-key Carouge has plenty of intimate, rustic bistros serving Swiss fare with a Mediterranean twist. Once a Sardinian enclave, the love of all things Italian persists: think antipasti, wood-fired pizza, risotto and fresh fish.

🔺 *Alfresco sustenance on the Place du Bourg de Four*

PICNIC SPOTS

Geneva has a string of attractive parks and gardens that are perfect for a picnic when the weather permits. Top choices include the Jardin Anglais and Bain des Pâquis pier, where you can lay your blanket by the lake front and drink in views of the Jet d'Eau fountain, or munch your lunch beside the rhododendrons in the flower-strewn Jardin Botanique. In a city that loves its food, there is no shortage of *pâtisseries*, *fromageries* and wine shops from which to fill your basket either!

LOCAL SPECIALITIES

Alpine heartiness meets French finesse in Geneva's kitchen, where fresh, locally sourced ingredients are used. Fondue is a perennial favourite and lots of fun – skinny forks are used to dip bread into a bubbling pot of cheese or fruit into thick hot chocolate. Another tasty winter warmer is *rösti* (grated potatoes with onion and bacon). Carnivores should tuck into *longeole* (unsmoked pork sausage flavoured with cumin and fennel) or try *l'assiette valaisanne* (cold meat platter). Other specialities to look out for include lake perch, creamy Tomme cheese and artichoke-like cardoons.

WALKING ON CHOCOLATE

Chocolate is a firm favourite in Geneva, and every *chocolatier* sells the speciality of the city, *pavés glacés*. The brainchild of the 19th-century confectioner Henri Auer, these creamy chocolates shaped like cobblestones simply melt in your mouth.

Surrounded by vine-clad hills, Geneva is wine country, producing some excellent varieties including crisp Chasselas whites, full-bodied Gamay reds and fruity Pinot Noirs. Those that want to taste the grape where it is grown should make for the wineries in nearby Russin and Satigny.

TIPPING

Nearly all restaurants in Geneva include a service charge of 15 per cent, but it's normal to leave a small tip if you were pleased with the service. Locals tend to round off the bill to the nearest few francs or tip between 5 and 10 per cent. In Switzerland, it's standard practice to give the tip direct to the waiter.

USEFUL DINING PHRASES

I would like a table for ... people
Je voudrais une table pour ... personnes
Zher voodray ewn tabl poor ... pehrson

May I have the bill, please?
L'addition, s'il vous plaît!
Laddyssyawng, sylvooplay!

Waiter/waitress!
Monsieur/Mademoiselle, s'il vous plaît?
M'sewr/madmwahzel, sylvooplay!

Does it have meat in it?
Est-ce que ce plat contient de la viande?
Essker ser plah kontyang der lah veeahngd?

Where is the toilet please?
Où sont les toilettes, s'il vous plaît?
Oo sawng leh twahlaitt, sylvooplay?

Entertainment & nightlife

As the sun sets over Mont Blanc, neon lights and twinkling fountains illuminate the lake. While Geneva may not seem wild on the surface, dig deeper and you'll find it has more than enough after-dark action to keep night owls happy. With a lively student population that just wants to have fun, a plethora of ultra-cool lounge bars and underground clubs vying for your attention, this city knows how to let its hair down.

Variety is the spice of this city's nightlife – think divas, dressed up to the nines, sipping cocktails on the Quai du Mont Blanc and locals unwinding over a glass of red wine on a terrace in the Old Town; arty types hanging out in Plainpalais bars and fashionistas sharing the dance floor in Place de la Fusterie. From grunge to glitz, roulette to reggae, fine wines to perfect pints, Geneva will entertain you.

A night in Geneva begins in typically relaxed fashion with a good meal in one of the Old Town's wood-panelled brasseries and a few drinks on the Quai du Mont Blanc. Things pick up around 23.00 as bars lining the Pâquis, Plainpalais and centre fill with high-spirited revellers, and the music is turned up a notch. If you want to shake your booty in one of the hottest clubs in town, don't get there until after midnight.

High culture, too, runs through Geneva's veins: from sopranos and strings at the opulent Grand Théâtre to live performances at L'Usine and Le Chat Noir. To book tickets in advance, contact the venue direct or try Billetnet, which covers major festivals, gigs and performances. ⓦ www.billetnet.ch

● *As darkness descends, Geneva lights up*

CLUBS

Geneva's clubbing scene moves from students bopping to urban beats to glamour-pusses sipping champagne as they strut their stuff. Check out the ultra-chic B Club and Platinum Glam Club (you might just get in if you look the part), Café Cuba where partygoers sway to Latino rhythms and 7ème Ciel for house music and Mojitos.

PERFORMING ARTS

Classical concerts, opera and dance raise the roof on the Place Neuve, which is dominated by the acclaimed Grand Théâtre and Conservatoire de Musique. For a more offbeat experience, make for funky Le Chat Noir in Carouge, which reels in the crowds with live jazz and jam sessions in the cellar. Or try L'Usine, a former factory that now churns out cutting-edge performances. The Arena is the place for everything from stand-up comedy to musicals and rock concerts.

PUBS & BARS

The buzzing Place du Bourg de Four is the place for alfresco drinking and people watching in summer. For snug British-style pubs with no frills, a laid-back feel and Guinness on tap, make for the Grand Rue or Rue de Lausanne. The Plainpalais district around Rue Bovy-Lysberg and Place du Cirque is the Left Bank's hip heart, serving up Zen-style lounge bars where the cocktails are creative, grooves mellow and crowds effortlessly cool.

    If you're seeking trendy rather than traditional, you'll get your kicks in the multicultural Pâquis on the Right Bank. Clustered here are hole-in-the-wall bars playing everything from

soul to salsa, and the vibe is very much come as you are. While this is Geneva's red-light district, it's unlikely you'll feel threatened walking here at night.

ENTERTAINMENT LISTINGS

Geneva Agenda This online booklet gives up-to-date listings of events in Geneva. Ⓦ www.geneve-tourisme.ch

Info Concert Find the latest festival, concert, theatre and cinema listings on this French site. Ⓦ www.infoconcert.com

⬥ *The Grand Théâtre dominates Place Neuve*

Sport & relaxation

SPECTATOR SPORTS

With a capacity of 30,000, Stade de Genève is home to the city's biggest football club, Servette and host stadium for three European Championship matches in 2008. **ⓐ** 16 Route des Jeunes **ⓣ** 022 827 44 00 **ⓦ** www.servettefc.ch **ⓝ** Bus: 21 or 22 to Stade de Genève

The multi-purpose arena at Geneva's huge Palexpo Exhibition Centre, which is situated next to the airport, hosts a number of top sporting events including the Showjumping World Cup. **ⓐ** Grand-Saconnex **ⓣ** 022 761 11 11 **ⓦ** www.palexpo.ch **ⓝ** Bus: 5, 10, 18 to Palexpo

PARTICIPATION SPORTS

Adventure Center

From kayaking the rapids of the Arve River to paragliding from Mont Salève, this professional centre has 50 years' experience and offers bags of white-knuckle thrills. There are guides for the inexperienced or you can hire craft if you prefer to head off on your own adventure. **ⓐ** 8 Quai des Vernets **ⓣ** 079 213 41 40 **ⓦ** www.rafting.ch **ⓔ** info@rafting.ch **ⓛ** Apr–Oct; closed Nov–Mar **ⓝ** Tram: 15, 17 to Acacias

Swimming

Geneva has plenty of indoor pools, but when the weather warms, head for the lake. Make a splash from the Bain des Pâquis pier, or go to Geneva's beach. Genève-Plage is set in a large park on the lake edge, and has an Olympic-sized pool, waterslides, diving boards, volleyball, basketball and children's activities. ⓐ Quai de Cologny ⓣ 022 736 24 82 ⓦ www.geneve-plage.ch ⓛ 10.00–20.00 May–Sept; closed Oct–Apr ⓝ Bus: 2, E, G to Genève-Plage. Admission charge

Watersports

The Wake Sport Centre next to Geneva's beach provides waterskiing, wakeboarding, wakeskating and hydrofoiling. ⓐ 9 Quai de Cologny ⓣ 079 202 38 73 ⓦ www.wake.ch ⓛ May–Sept; closed Oct–Apr ⓝ Bus: 2, E, G to Genève-Plage

RELAXATION
Cable-car

Take the cable-car (*téléphérique*) to Geneva's nearest mountain, 1,380-m (4,527-ft) Mont Salève, where you can hike or mountain bike in summer and cross-country ski in winter. There is also a playground at the top to entertain the kids. The views are spectacular. ⓐ Veyrier ⓣ 04 50 39 86 86 ⓛ 09.30–18.00 Tues–Sun; closed Mon ⓝ Bus: 8, 34, 41 to Veyrier-École

Cruise

Swissboat offer an array of relaxing mini-cruises to take in the sights, as well as trips along the River Rhône. ⓐ 4–8 Quai du Mont-Blanc ⓣ 022 732 47 47 ⓦ www.swissboat.com ⓝ Bus: 29 to Chantepoulet

Accommodation

Swiss hotels are notoriously pricey, but it is also possible to find central hotels that won't break the bank. There's also a good range of character accommodation available in Geneva, including Swiss-chalet, Belle Époque, feng-shui-inspired and boutique-style hotels. The city's hostels offer great value for solo travellers, while campers can enjoy prime lake views.

HOTELS

Hôtel Bel'Espérance £ A central, no-frills hotel. All rooms have satellite TV and the terrace has views over the city's rooftops to Lake Geneva. ⓐ 1 Rue de la Vallée ⓣ 022 818 37 37 ⓕ 022 818 37 73 ⓦ www.hotel-bel-esperance.ch Ⓝ Tram: 16 to Rive

Hôtel Bernina £ Conveniently located opposite the station, this hotel has basic but spotless rooms that won't blow the budget, all with cable TV, safe and soundproofed windows. ⓐ 22 Place Cornavin ⓣ 022 908 49 50 ⓕ 022 908 49 51 ⓦ www.bernina-geneve.ch Ⓝ Train: Gare Cornavin

Hôtel de Genève £ A stone's throw from Geneva's key sights, this Belle Époque hotel scores points for its homely feel. The wood-

> **PRICE RATING**
> The ratings below indicate the approximate cost of a room for two people for one night in Geneva.
> **£** up to CHF150   **££** CHF150–250   **£££** over CHF250

panelled reception recalls an alpine chalet and the rooms are well kept. ⓐ 1 Place Isaac-Mercier ⓣ 022 732 32 64 ⓕ 022 732 82 64 ⓦ www.hotel-de-geneve.ch ⓝ Tram: 15, 16 to Isaac-Mercier

Hôtel de la Cloche £ This intimate, family-run hotel is very central. The 19th-century townhouse has old-world charm with wood floors, a fireplace and cosy rooms – ask for one with a view of the lake. ⓐ 6 Rue de la Cloche ⓣ 022 732 94 81 ⓔ hotelcloche@freesurf.ch ⓝ Bus: 1 to Monthoux

Hôtel des Tourelles £ Overlooking the River Rhône, this charming little hotel has attractive rooms with high ceilings, soft drapes and hardwood floors. ⓐ 2 Boulevard James-Fazy ⓣ 022 732 44 23 ⓕ 022 732 76 20 ⓦ www.destourelles.ch ⓔ hotel@destourelles.ch ⓝ Tram: 16 to Isaac-Mercier

Hôtel Admiral ££ This mid-range hotel offers smart rooms decorated in warm hues. Perks include free wireless internet and a hearty breakfast. ⓐ 8 Rue Rossi ⓣ 022 906 97 00 ⓕ 022 906 97 01 ⓦ www.hoteladmiral.ch ⓔ info@hoteladmiral.ch ⓝ Train: Gare Cornavin

Hôtel Edelweiss ££ Reminiscent of a traditional Swiss chalet, this hotel brings the mountains to the heart of Geneva. The snug rooms have all mod cons. ⓐ 2 Place de la Navigation ⓣ 022 544 51 51 ⓕ 022 544 51 99 ⓦ www.manotel.com ⓔ edelweiss@manotel.com ⓝ Bus: 1 to Navigation

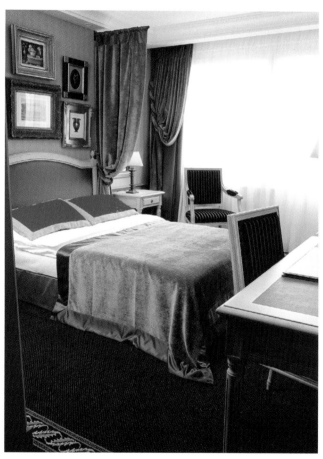

◐ *Wallow in luxury at the Manotel Royal*

Hôtel Jade ££ Earthy tones create a sense of calm in this feng-shui-inspired hotel near the lake. ⓐ 55 Rue Rothschild ⓣ 022 544 38 38 ⓕ 022 544 38 99 ⓦ www.manotel.com ⓝ Tram: 13 to Butini

Hôtel Longemalle ££ With high ceilings, dark wood floors and ornate flourishes, this hotel epitomises Belle Époque elegance. The attractive rooms offer minibar, cable TV and internet access. ⓐ 13 Place Longemalle ⓣ 022 818 62 62 ⓕ 022 818 62 61 ⓦ www.longemalle.ch ⓔ info@longemalle.ch ⓝ Bus: 27 to Place du Port

Hôtel Tiffany £££ This turn-of-the-century boutique hotel is a real find; the plush rooms all have squeaky-clean bathrooms. Relax in the wood-panelled lounge, book a massage and wake up to an excellent breakfast. ⓐ 1 Rue des Marbiers ⓣ 022 708 16 16 ⓕ 022 708 16 17 ⓦ www.hotel-tiffany.ch ⓔ info@hotel-tiffany.ch ⓝ Tram: 16 to Stand

Manotel Royal £££ Contemporary chic sums up this smart hotel offering 24-hour room service, free wireless internet access and onsite parking. After a long day of sightseeing, unwind in the *hammam* and sauna, or enjoy drinks by the fireside in the lounge. ⓐ 41 Rue de Lausanne ⓣ 022 906 14 14 ⓕ 022 906 14 99 ⓦ www.manotel.com ⓔ info@manotel.com ⓝ Tram: 13, 15 to Môle

HOSTELS
City Hostel £ Near the main station, this offers single, double and dorm beds. The rooms are clean and there's a communal

kitchen, lockers, a TV room and internet access. ⓐ 2 Rue Ferrier
ⓣ 022 901 15 00 ⓕ 022 901 15 60 ⓦ www.cityhostel.ch
ⓔ info@cityhostel.ch ⓝ Tram: 13 to Môle

YH Geneva £ The pick of the budget bunch, this bright and
modern hostel has clean and comfortable shared dorms. The
good facilities include a laundry, snack bar, internet access and
library. Breakfast is included. ⓐ 28–30 Rue Rothschild
ⓣ 022 732 62 60 ⓕ 022 738 39 87 ⓦ www.yh-geneva.ch
ⓔ booking@yh-geneva.ch ⓝ Bus: 1 to Gautier

CAMPSITES
Camping du Val de l'Allondon £ Situated in a nature reserve, this
peaceful campsite is just a short train ride from the centre.
ⓐ 106 Route de l'Ilondon, Satigny ⓣ 022 753 15 15 ⓕ 022 753 15 55
ⓦ www.camp-allondon.ch ⓔ camp.allondon@bluewin.ch
ⓛ Apr–Oct; closed Nov–Mar ⓝ Train: to Satigny

Camping Pointe à la Bise £ Enjoy breakfast on the beach at this
lakefront site, 10 minutes' drive from Geneva. The camping
ground has shady pitches and facilities include a swimming
pool, bike hire, restaurant and shop. ⓐ 18 Chemin de la Bise,
Vésenaz ⓣ 022 752 12 96 ⓕ 022 752 37 67 ⓦ www.campingtcs.ch
ⓛ Apr–Sept; closed Oct–Mar ⓝ Bus: E to La Bise

THE BEST OF GENEVA

There's plenty to enjoy in Geneva, but these are the sights that should really not be missed.

TOP 10 ATTRACTIONS

- **Cathédrale St Pierre (St Peter's Cathedral)** Scale the North Tower's spiral staircase and see Geneva shrink (see page 60).

- **Bains des Pâquis** Hang out with the hip crowd on the Right Bank's pier (see page 76).

- **MAMCO (Museum of Contemporary Art)** Contemporary art is on the menu at this funky Left Bank gallery (see page 68).

- **Le Chat Noir** The cat's out of the bag – this club is *the* coolest place in Carouge (see page 101).

- **Jet d'Eau (Water Fountain)** This 140-m (460-ft) fountain rises like a vision above Lake Geneva (see page 64).

- **Musée d'Art et d'Histoire (Art & History Museum)** This cavernous museum has everything from paintings by Monet to Egyptian artefacts (see page 68).

- **Horloge Fleurie (Floral Clock)** Created from 6,500 flowers, this celebrates the Swiss tradition of watch- and clock-making (see page 60).

- **Palais des Nations (Palace of Nations)** Take a tour of this political powerhouse (see page 80).

- **Jardin Botanique (Botanical Gardens)** Mediterranean blooms and pink flamingos vie for attention at these gorgeous lakefront gardens (see page 77).

- **Musée Internationale de la Croix Rouge (International Red Cross Museum)** The work of the world's most famous humanitarian organisation is explored at this fascinating museum (see page 83).

The view from the cathedral platform

HALF-DAY: GENEVA IN A HURRY

Kick off your stay with a whirlwind tour of the hilltop Old Town, winding through narrow streets to take in key sights like the arcaded town hall and turreted Maison Tavel. Pause at the medieval Cathédrale St Pierre to climb the North Tower for giddying views over the city's rooftops and lake. Before you leave, be sure to glimpse the flower-strewn Horloge Fleurie and dancing Jet d'Eau from the manicured lawns of the Jardin Anglais.

1 DAY: TIME TO SEE A LITTLE MORE

A stroll along the lakefront brings you to the vibrant Bains des Pâquis pier, where (weather permitting) you can take a quick dip or drink in views of snow-clad Mont Blanc over a coffee. Further along, you'll reach Mon Repos villa and the beautiful Jardin Botanique, where pink flamingos wade. Back on the Left Bank, munch on rösti beneath the Taverne de la Madeleine's beams, then head for the Musée d'Art et d'Histoire to admire Van Gogh masterpieces and the famous Konrad Witz altarpiece.

2–3 DAYS: SHORT CITY-BREAK

Scratch the city's surface to find lesser-known treasures – from cutting-edge exhibitions at MAMCO to the lofty Mur des Réformateurs in the Parc des Bastions. After taking a tour of the Palace of Nations, pop across to the International Red Cross Museum, which tells a moving tale of triumph and tragedy. Next up, Carouge beckons, with its Sardinian-style houses, pavement cafés and kooky boutiques that are a world away from the buzzing centre. As night falls, catch quirky performances at L'Usine or a live music act at Carouge's Le Chat Noir.

LONGER: ENJOYING GENEVA TO THE FULL

Once you've devoured all Geneva has to offer, get a taste for the surrounding region. Cross the Franco-Swiss border to Annecy, where canals flow to the red-turreted medieval castle. Here you can try your hand at mountain climbing or drift away on the lake's translucent waters.

Stepping east, enjoy the delights of the Olympic city of Lausanne – from the Gothic heights of Notre-Dame Cathedral via the art gems gracing the walls of the grand Palais de Rumine to the relaxed vibe on the waterfront promenade of Ouchy.

△ *Head along the lakefront to buzzing Bains des Pâquis*

Something for nothing

Switzerland has quite a reputation for being expensive, so it's pleasing to discover that some of the best things in Geneva are free. First up is a whirlwind tour of the Old Town that won't cost you a penny (or a Swiss franc, to be precise), where an amble takes in sights such as the arcaded Hôtel de Ville, frescoed Tour du Molard and the medieval Cathédrale St Pierre – step inside to admire the magnificent rose window. Wind through narrow cobbled streets to the water's edge, where the Horloge Fleurie keeps ticking and the Jet d'Eau fountain turns heads.

For a free taste of local life, head for the shady Parc des Bastions, where people congregate to play chess on giant boards and the Mur des Réformateurs commemorates key figures of the Reformation. In summer, bring your swimming togs and take a dip from Bains des Pâquis pier. This may be a city, but there's plenty of country about: explore Geneva's patchwork of greenery by strolling the Right Bank's promenade. From here you can glimpse sculpture-strewn gardens and gaze at one of the city's most striking sights – the sun setting over Mont Blanc. You can easily spend the afternoon wandering through the vast Jardin Botanique, home to cactuses, fragrant plants and deer.

If all that exercise has made you thirsty, be sure to pick up a leaflet from the tourist office giving a comprehensive list of wineries offering free tastings every Saturday. For the cost of a bus ticket, you could vine-hop your way around the wine-growing villages of Anières, Céligny, Russin and Satigny.

It costs nothing to get your cultural fix in many of Geneva's intoxicating galleries and museums. Art buffs should make a beeline for the Musée d'Art et d'Histoire to brush up against Rembrandts and Roman treasures, or the sublime Musée Ariana to gawp at precious porcelain. Savvy travellers time their visit to coincide with the first Sunday of the month, when most museums are free, including the must-see MAMCO and Musée Rath.

⬥ *Musée Ariana: see the ceramic collection for free*

When it rains

When the rain comes, Geneva shines, with a host of indoor activities to help you forget about the wet weather. If you feel like hibernating, the Old Town has a glut of cosy cafés and low-beamed bistros that are just the ticket. And no country does comfort food like the Swiss – everything seems much brighter over a mug of real hot chocolate or a *caquelon* filled with cheese fondue to warm your cockles. When the heavens open, the arty cafés around Plainpalais are a great place to hang out with a bottomless cup of coffee and a good book.

Undercover shopping can be the ultimate pick-me-up when it rains. To escape sudden showers, scoot into central Globus on Rue du Rhône to immerse yourself in the latest styles and tasty specialities in the basement food court. A stone's throw from Carouge, modern La Praille mall shelters 80 high-street shops from Morgan fashion to Martel pralines, plus a plethora of tea rooms, restaurants and a bowling alley. Ⓦ www.la-praille.ch

Culture can compensate for dull skies, too. Go down instead of up at the cathedral to view centuries-old foundations at the archaeological site. A few paces away, the medieval Maison Tavel traces Geneva's history with elaborate art and artefacts. Immerse yourself in contemporary creations at MAMCO, then pop over to the elegant Musée Patek Philippe to gawp at art nouveau timepieces. Escape heavy downpours at the heart-rending Musée Internationale de la Croix Rouge to learn more about the humanitarian work of this international organisation.

It may be too nippy for a dip in the lake, but that's all the more excuse to test out the state-of-the-art *hammam* and

sauna complex at the Bain des Pâquis. A long steam in the
Turkish bath or a soothing massage will leave you feeling as fresh
as a daisy. If you've got cash to splash, the ultimate boost on a
drizzly day is a trip to the exclusive La Réserve spa, which has a
huge range of feel-good therapies to chase away rainy-day blues.

🔹 *A temple to timekeeping*

On arrival

TIME DIFFERENCES

Like the rest of Switzerland, Geneva runs on Central European time (CET), an hour ahead of Greenwich Mean Time (CET) and two hours ahead during Daylight Savings Time (end Mar–end Oct). In the summer, at 12.00, time elsewhere is as follows:

Australia Eastern Standard Time 20.00, Central Standard Time 19.30, Western Standard Time 18.00

New Zealand 22.00

South Africa 12.00

UK & Republic of Ireland 11.00

US & Canada Newfoundland Time 07.30, Atlantic Canada Time 07.00, Eastern Standard Time 06.00, Central Time 05.00, Mountain Time 04.00, Pacific Time 03.00, Alaska 02.00

ARRIVING

By air

A major international hub, Aéroport Genève-Cointrin (GVA) is 5 km (3 miles) from the centre. It is the base for more than 70 airlines flying to 90 destinations including London, New York, Paris and Rome. easyJet and bmibaby offer some of the best budget flights. Other key airlines include British Airways, American Airlines, Swiss, KLM and Virgin Express.

The modern airport offers an excellent range of facilities open seven days a week, including shops, cafés, ATMs, car hire, a post office, supermarket and pharmacy.

A train shuttles passengers between the airport and Geneva's main station in just eight minutes (trains depart every

15 minutes). Alternatively you can take bus number 10 into town, which departs every 10 minutes. The Unireso information desk in the arrivals hall provides tickets and details on routes and timetables. A taxi to the centre will set you back about CHF35. **ⓐ** 21 Route de l'Aeroport **ⓣ** 022 717 71 11 **ⓕ** 022 798 43 77 **ⓦ** www.gva.ch

By bus

The city's central bus station, Gare Routière, is situated on Place Dorcière. A number of long-distance buses depart from here, serving international destinations including Lyon, Rome and London. **ⓐ** Place Dorcière **ⓣ** 022 732 02 30 **ⓦ** www.gare-routiere.ch

By car

Geneva is well connected to the rest of Switzerland and Europe via the A40 (L'Autoroute Blanche) to the French Alps, the A42 to Lyon, and the A1 to Lausanne. For the centre, follow the signs for Genève-Lac and the Route de Lausanne.

Although driving in Geneva is relatively hassle-free compared to other major cities, parking can be expensive and difficult to find. Plan in advance by checking the location of multistorey and P&R car parks. **ⓦ** www.geneve.ch. The speed limit is strictly observed in Switzerland and you should display a *Vignette* (toll sticker) in the windscreen at all times.

By rail

Swiss Federal Railways (SBB) are renowned for their efficiency and comfort, and operate a regular service to Swiss cities

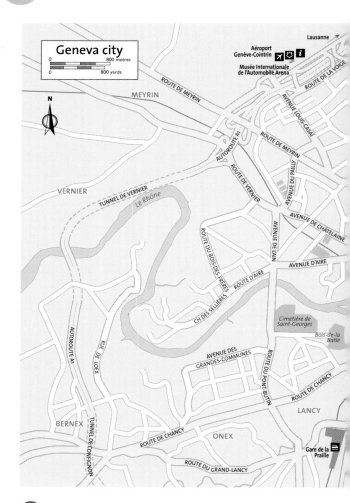

Geneva city

0 800 metres
0 800 yards

Lausanne

Aéroport
Genève-Cointrin

Musée Internationale
de l'Automobile Arena

N

ROUTE DE MEYRIN

MEYRIN

ROUTE DE LA VOIE

AVENUE LOUIS-CASAÏ

AUTOROUTE A1

ROUTE DE MEYRIN

ROUTE DE VERNIER

AVENUE DU PAILLY

VERNIER

TUNNEL DE VERNIER

Le Rhône

AVENUE DE CHÂTELAINE

ROUTE DU BOIS-DES-FRÈRES

AVENUE DE L'AIN

ROUTE D'AIRE

AVENUE D'AIRE

CH DES SELLIÈRES

Cimetière de
Saint-Georges

Bois-de-la
Batie

AUTOROUTE A1

RUE DE LOËX

AVENUE DES
GRANDES-COMMUNES

ROUTE DU PONT-BUTIN

ROUTE DE CHANCY

LANCY

BERNEX

TUNNEL DE CONFIGNON

ROUTE DE CHANCY

ONEX

Gare de la
Praille

ROUTE DU GRAND-LANCY

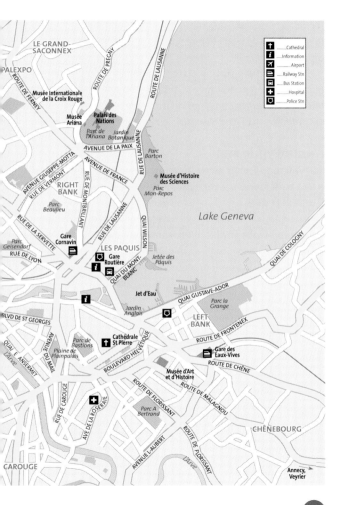

✝	Cathedral
𝑖	Information
✈	Airport
🚆	Railway Stn
🚌	Bus Station
✚	Hospital
Ⓞ	Police Stn

LE-GRAND-SACONNEX

PALEXPO

ROUTE DE PREGNY

ROUTE DE LAUSANNE

Musée Internationale
de la Croix Rouge

ROUTE DE FERNEY

Musée
Ariana

Palais des
Nations

Parc de
l'Ariana

Jardin
Botanique

AVENUE DE LA PAIX

Parc
Barton

AVENUE GIUSEPPE-MOTTA

RUE DE VERMONT

AVENUE DE FRANCE

RUE DE MONTBRILLANT

RUE DE LAUSANNE

Musée d'Histoire
des Sciences

Parc
Mon-Repos

RIGHT
BANK

Parc
Beaulieu

Lake Geneva

RUE DE LA SERVETTE

Parc
Geisendorf

Gare
Cornavin

RUE DE LYON

LES PAQUIS

Gare
Routière

𝑖

QUAI DU MONT-BLANC

QUAI WILSON

QUAI DE COLOGNY

Jetée des
Pâquis

Jet d'Eau

QUAI GUSTAVE-ADOR

Parc la
Grange

𝑖

BLVD DE ST GEORGES

Jardin
Anglais

Ⓞ

LEFT
BANK

ROUTE DE FRONTENEX

AVENUE DU MAIL

QUAI E. ANSERMET

L'Arve

Parc de
Bastions

Plaine de
Plainpalais

Cathédrale
St-Pierre

BOULEVARD HELVÉTIQUE

Gare des
Eaux-Vives

ROUTE DE CHÊNE

Musée d'Art
et d'Histoire

RUE DE CAROUGE

✚

AVE DE LA ROSERAIE

ROUTE DE FLORISSANT

Parc A
Bertrand

ROUTE DE MALAGNOU

CHÊNEBOURG

CAROUGE

AVENUE L-AUBERT

ROUTE DE FLORISSANT

L'Arve

Annecy,
Veyrier

including Lausanne (45 minutes), Bern (2 hours) and Zurich
(3 hours); in addition to French destinations like Lyon (2 hours)
and Paris (3 hours).

The main train station, Gare Cornavin, is located on the Right
Bank and has a good range of facilities including left luggage,
bureau de change and a post office. **ⓐ** Place Cornavin
ⓣ 0900 300 300 **ⓦ** www.cff.ch

FINDING YOUR FEET

You will soon feel at home in Geneva, a cosmopolitan city with
a laid-back feel and a pedestrianised Old Town. Many locals are
fluent in English and happy to direct travellers.

As Geneva is a safe city with a low crime rate, it's unlikely
you'll experience any problems during your stay, but it's always
wise to keep an eye on your valuables and be careful if walking
through dimly lit, less-populated areas at night.

ORIENTATION

Hemmed in by the Alps and straddling the Franco-Swiss border,
Geneva is located in Switzerland's southwest corner. Split in two

---

IF YOU GET LOST, TRY ...

Do you speak English?   **Is this the way to...?**
Parlez-vous anglais?   C'est la bonne direction pour...?
Pahrlayvoo ahnglay?   *Seh lah bon deerekseeawng poor...?*
Can you point to it on my map?
Pouvez-vous me le montrer sur la carte?
Poovehvoo mer ler mawngtreh sewr lah kart?

by the snaking River Rhône, the city hugs the banks of Lake Geneva and is framed by mountains.

Most of the action centres around the lake: the UN institutions, Jardin Botanique and Les Pâquis on the Right Bank and Cathédrale St Pierre, the Jet d'Eau fountain and the Plainpalais on the Left. Carouge is just south of the centre.

GETTING AROUND

Geneva's efficient public transport network makes it simple to get around. If you're making several trips, it's worth picking up a 48- or 72-hour Geneva Transport Card from the tourist office for unlimited use of the city's trams, buses, boats and trains.

By bike

Geneva encourages pedal power, and from May to October bikes can be borrowed for free. The Genève Roule website provides more details. ⓦ www.geneveroule.ch

○ *The action in Geneva centres around the lake*

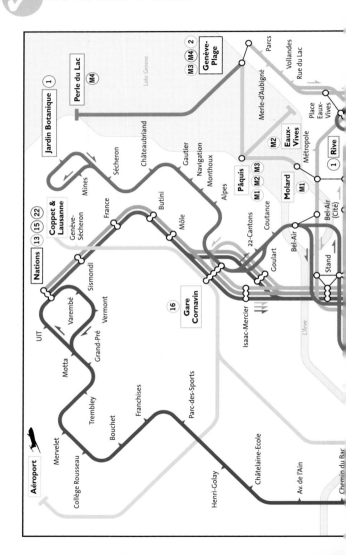

By boat

Hop aboard one of the yellow-and-white ferries (*mouettes*), which shuttle passengers every 10 minutes between Pâquis, Eaux-Vives and Place du Molard. ⓦ www.swissboat.com

By bus

Geneva's dependable bus network operates from 06.00 to 24.00 with a night service at weekends. You'll find route maps and timetables at each stop. ⓦ www.noctambus.ch

By tram

Fast and reliable, Geneva's four tram lines crisscross the city and operate from 06.00 to 24.00. Each stop has a ticket machine, for which you'll need exact change.

CAR HIRE

Geneva's excellent public transport network means you can get around easily. However, if you're planning on going further afield, hiring a car could be a good option.

Avis ⓐ 44 Rue de Lausanne ⓣ 022 731 90 00 ⓦ www.avis.com
ⓛ 07.30–18.45 Mon–Fri; 07.30–12.30, 13.30–17.00 Sat; closed Sun
Budget ⓐ Geneva Airport Arrivals Hall ⓣ 022 717 86 75
ⓦ www.budget.com ⓛ 08.00–23.00 Mon–Sun
Europcar ⓐ Geneva Airport Arrivals Hall ⓣ 022 717 81 10
ⓕ 022 788 36 70 ⓦ www.europcar.com ⓛ 07.00–23.30 Mon–Sun
Hertz ⓐ Geneva Airport Arrivals Hall ⓣ 022 717 80 80
ⓕ 022 788 24 05 ⓦ www.hertz.com ⓛ 07.00–23.30 Mon–Sun

ⓞ *Committed to peace: a statue near the Palais des Nations*

Left Bank

If you're looking for variety, Geneva's Left Bank will not disappoint: from the medieval Old Town in the shadow of the cathedral spires to the glittering lakefront where the Floral Clock ticks and the Plainpalais and its ultra-cool bars. Whether you want to chill in shady parks, wallow in modern art, gorge on fondue or boutique-shop along Grand Rue, you can graze for days on the Left Bank's riches.

SIGHTS & ATTRACTIONS

Cathédrale St Pierre (St Peter's Cathedral)

The medieval monolith rises like a vision above Geneva's Old Town. The edifice is a fusion of Romanesque, Gothic and neoclassical styles – step inside to admire its cross-ribbed vaulting and huge rose window. Underground is an archaeological site that traces the cathedral's early foundations. But if you're seeking highs, climb the North Tower's steep spiral staircase to view the bell tower and spires. The terrace affords bird's-eye views over the city's rooftops, lake and mountains. ⓐ 6 Cour St Pierre ⓞ 022 319 71 91 ⓦ www.saintpierre-geneve.ch ⓛ 09.30–18.30 Mon–Sat, 12.00–18.30 Sun (summer); 10.00–17.30 Mon–Sat, 12.00–17.30 Sun (winter) ⓑ Bus: 36 to Cathédrale. Admission charge (North Tower)

Horloge Fleurie (Floral Clock)

A living tribute to a country that runs like clockwork, this blooming beautiful clock in the Jardin Anglais will have you

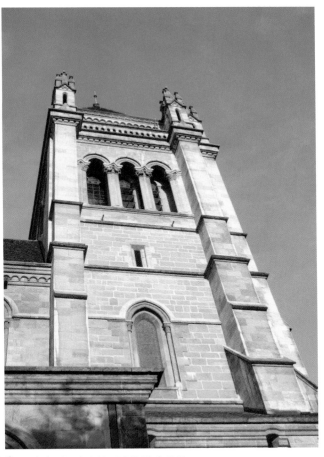

◆ *Reach the dizzy heights at Cathédrale St Pierre*

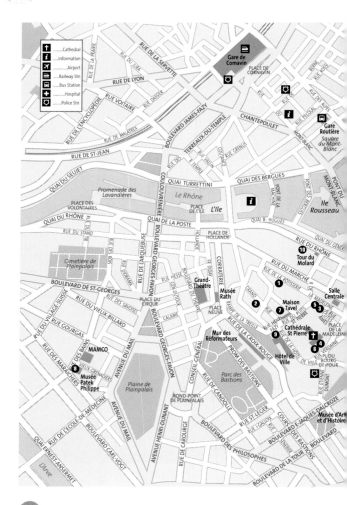

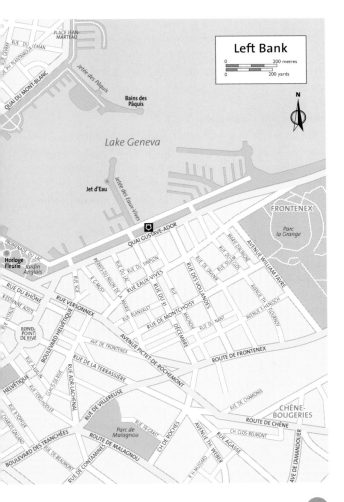

Left Bank

0 ——————— 200 metres
0 ——————— 200 yards

N

PLACE JEAN-MARTEAU

RUE DU LÉMAN

RUE PH. PLANTAMOUR

RUE DU CARAN

QUAI DU MONT-BLANC

Jetée des Pâquis

Bains des Pâquis

Lake Geneva

Jet d'Eau

Jetée des Eaux-Vives

FRONTENEX

Parc la Grange

QUAI GUSTAVE-ADOR

PROMENADE DU LAC

Horloge Fleurie

Jardin Anglais

RUE DU LAC

PIERRE-FATIO

RUE DU SIMPLON

RUE EAUX-VIVES

RUE DU 31

MARIE DUBOIS

RUE DU CLOS

AVENUE WILLIAM FAVRE

RUE DE LA MAIRIE

E. CAMUSY

RUE DES VOLLANDES

RUE SILLEM

AVENUE TH. FLOURNOY

RUE DU RHÔNE

RUE SCIE

RUE VERSONNEX

RUE BLANVALET

RUE DE MONTCHOISY

DÉCEMBRE

MALAGNOU

RUE DU NANT

AVENUE E.H. ENISCH

RUE D'ITALIE

R. ÉTIENNE AOSTE

ROND-POINT DE RIVE

BOULEVARD HELVÉTIQUE

AVENUE PICTET-DE-ROCHEMONT

AVE DE FRONTENEX

ROUTE DE FRONTENEX

HELVÉTIQUE

R. ALULIN

RUE DE LA TERRASSIÈRE

R. FERDHOPFER

RUE ADRI-LACHENAL

GLACIS-DE-RIVE

AVE DE CHAMONIX

CHÊNE-BOUGERIES

R. OFFER

CHARLES-GALLAND

RUE DE VILLEREUSE

RUE FR.CRAST

ROUTE DE CHÊNE

CH. CLOS-BELMONT

RUE AGASSE

BOULEVARD DES TRANCHÉES

RUE DE BEAUMONT

Parc de Malagnou

CH. DE ROCHES

ROUTE DE MALAGNOU

AVENUE TH. WEBER

RUE DE CONTAMINES

F. H. MUSSARD

AVE DE L'AMANDOLIER

63

reaching for your camera. Around 6,500 brightly coloured flowers and plants are used to create new displays each spring and autumn to celebrate Switzerland's famous watch-making industry.
ⓐ Jardin Anglais, Quai du Général-Guisan Ⓝ Bus: 27 to Place du Port

Hôtel de Ville (Town Hall)

With its arcades overlooking a cobbled inner courtyard, Geneva's town hall has been the cogs and wheels of the city's political life since the 15th century and is still the seat of the cantonal government. Just opposite, take a peek at the Old Arsenal, a former granary with impressive canons and mosaic frescoes depicting historical scenes.
ⓐ Rue de l'Hôtel-de-Ville Ⓝ Bus: 36 to Hôtel de Ville

Jardin Anglais (English Garden)

This ever-so-English garden is laced with paths that pass dancing fountains, statues and a bandstand. Find a shady spot beneath the oak trees, take a cruise on the lake or wander along the front for uninterrupted views of the fountain. In summer, the park is awash with magnolias.
ⓐ Quai du Général-Guisan Ⓝ Bus: 27 to Place du Port

Jet d'Eau (Water Fountain)

Perhaps Geneva's most iconic landmark, this eye-catching 140-m (460-ft)-high fountain cascades into Lake Geneva when the weather is fine and looks particularly striking illuminated by night.
ⓐ Quai du Général-Guisan Ⓝ Bus: E, G to Eaux-Vives

WATERWORKS

Now the focal point of the lake, Geneva's famous Jet d'Eau was originally just a security valve. Over the years the locals grew quite attached to this huge fountain – one of the largest in the world. Today it shoots around 500 litres (132 gallons) of water per second into the sky and, when the sun shines, creates a rainbow that can best be admired from the Pont du Mont Blanc bridge.

◯ *Splashing success: the Jet d'Eau*

Mur des Réformateurs (Reformation Wall)

This breathtaking, 100-m (330-ft)-long wall was built in 1909 to commemorate Jean Calvin. Set against a backdrop of bas-reliefs are four larger-than-life sculptures that represent the key figures of the 16th-century Reformation.

🅐 Parc des Bastions 🚊 Tram: 12, 17 to Place Neuve

🔺 *Chill out with the locals*

Parc des Bastions

Originally part of the city's fortifications, this park is where locals come to jog along the tree-lined avenue, play chess on giant boards and relax in the sunshine. This central pocket of greenery is home to one of the main university buildings and the awe-inspiring Reformation Wall.

ⓐ Parc des Bastions ⓣ 022 418 50 00 ⓝ Tram: 12, 17 to Place Neuve

Tour du Molard (Molard Tower)

Once part of the city's defence walls, today this red-turreted tower is dwarfed by the centre's taller buildings. Glance up to see its frescoes, clock face and coat of arms.

ⓐ Place du Molard ⓝ Tram: 16 to Molard

CULTURE

Grand Théâtre (Opera House)

Dominating Place Neuve square, this grand 19th-century opera house has earned an international reputation for its world-class opera, theatre, ballet and recitals. The season runs from October to May.

ⓐ 3 Place Neuve ⓣ 022 418 31 30 ⓕ 022 418 30 01
ⓦ www.geneveopera.ch ⓝ Tram: 12, 17 to Place Neuve

Maison Tavel

Set in the city's oldest medieval residence, this fascinating museum features displays of antique furniture, tapestries and silverware spanning the Middle Ages to the 20th century. Be sure to look at the model of pre-1850 Geneva.

6 Rue du Puits St Pierre 022 418 37 00 www.ville-ge.ch
 10.00–17.00 Tues–Sun; closed Mon Tram: 16 to Molard.
Admission charge

MAMCO (Museum of Contemporary Art)

This former factory is now the driving force behind Geneva's
contemporary art scene, presenting fresh and edgy temporary
exhibitions that focus on artists like John M Armleder and a
broad variety of mediums.
 10 Rue des Vieux-Grenadiers 022 320 61 22
 www.mamco.ch mamco@mamco.ch 12.00–18.00
Tues–Fri, 11.00–18.00 Sun, closed Mon Bus: 1 to École-
Médecine. Admission charge

Musée d'Art et d'Histoire (Art & History Museum)

A must-see for culture vultures, this cavernous museum covers fine
arts, archaeology and applied arts, presenting everything from
Egyptian antiquities to Roman pottery and medieval weaponry.
Art lovers should head straight for the permanent collection of
masterpieces from the likes of Rembrandt, Monet and Van Gogh.
A highlight is Konrad Witz's 15th-century altarpiece.
 2 Rue Charles-Galland 022 418 26 00 10.00–17.00
Tues–Sun; closed Mon Bus: 1, 7 to Rive

Musée Patek Philippe (Patek Philippe Museum)

A temple to Swiss timekeeping, this opulent museum shelters a
peerless collection of antique and Patek Philippe timepieces,
from elaborate 17th-century pocket watches to art nouveau
pendant designs and astronomical clocks.

ⓐ 7 Rue des Vieux-Grenadiers ⓣ 022 809 07 10
ⓦ www.patekmuseum.com ⓛ 14.00–17.00 Tues–Fri, 10.00–17.00
Sat, closed Sun & Mon ⓝ Bus: 1 to École-Médecine. Admission
charge

Musée Rath (Rath Museum)

Housed in a neoclassical building, this fine arts museum
showcases the collection of 19th-century benefactor Simon Rath
and frequently stages first-rate exhibitions.
ⓐ 2 Place Neuve ⓣ 022 418 33 40 ⓛ 10.00–17.00 Tues, Thur–Sun,
12.00–21.00 Wed, closed Mon ⓝ Tram: 12, 17 to Place Neuve.
Admission charge

Salle Centrale

If you're seeking an alternative cultural scene, this venue
screening art-house films and staging experimental
productions could be just the ticket. The centre's eclectic
programme stretches from flamenco to concerts, exhibitions
to improvised plays.
ⓐ 10 Rue de la Madeleine ⓣ 022 311 60 35 ⓦ www.sallecentrale.ch
ⓔ info@sallecentrale.ch ⓝ Bus: 11 to Sécheron

RETAIL THERAPY

Boulevard du Vin Sniff out Pinots and Sauvignon Blancs at this
sleek cellar where you can taste the wines before you buy.
ⓐ 1–3 Boulevard Georges-Favon ⓣ 022 310 91 90
ⓦ www.boulevard-du-vin.ch ⓛ 09.00–19.00 Mon–Fri,
10.00–18.00 Sat, closed Sun ⓝ Tram: 15 to Stand

THE CITY

Globus On the main shopping drag, this smart five-level department store has everything a shopaholic could desire: from fashion to sportswear, cosmetics and a glorious food court. ⓐ 48 Rue du Rhône ❶ 022 319 50 50 ⓛ 09.00–19.00 Mon–Wed, 09.00–21.00 Thur, 09.00–19.30 Fri, 09.00–18.00 Sat, closed Sun ⓛ Tram: 16 to Molard

Luci Mendola Handcrafted bangles, strings of beads and unusual rings fill this chic boutique. ⓐ 16 Rue de Verdaine ❶ 022 310 05 93 ⓦ www.luci-mendola.com ⓛ 14.00–18.30 Mon, 10.00–18.30 Tues, Thur & Fri, 11.00–18.30 Wed, 10.00–17.00 Sat, closed Sun ⓝ Bus: 27 to Place du Port

Plainpalais Flea Market Eagle-eyed bargain hunters spend the morning rummaging through antiques, vintage clothes, old records, books and bric-à-brac at this atmospheric flea market. ⓐ Plaine de Plainpalais ❶ 022 418 83 00 ⓛ 06.30–18.00 Wed & Sat ⓝ Tram: 12, 13 to Rond-Point de Plainpalais

Theodora Romance, nostalgia and the scent of lavender drift from this perfumer par excellence, where you'll find signature fragrances like Rosine rose perfumes and Santa Maria Novella eaux de toilette. ⓐ 37 Grand Rue ❶ 022 310 38 75 ⓦ www.parfumerietheodora.ch ⓛ 10.30–18.30 Tues, Wed & Fri, 10.30–19.30 Thur, 10.30–17.30 Sat, closed Sun & Mon ⓝ Bus: 29 to Molard

Zeller This dreamy *chocolatier* has a glass counter full of exquisite pralines, truffles, marzipan creations and melt-in-your-

mouth *pavés glacés* (cobblestone-shaped chocolates). It's a secret too sweet to keep... ⓐ 1 Place de Longemalle
☎ 022 311 50 26 🕐 08.00–18.45 Mon–Fri, 08.00–18.00 Sat, closed Sun Ⓝ Bus: 8, 27 to Place du Port

TAKING A BREAK

Alhambar £ ❶   Red velvet armchairs, art deco lamps and spacey lighting make this a top choice for Sunday brunch, fresh salads or filling pasta dishes. By night, the vintage-style café becomes a lively bar attracting a cool crowd. ⓐ 10 Rue de la Rôtisserie ☎ 022 312 13 13 Ⓦ www.alhambar.com 🕐 12.00–14.00 Mon & Sat, 12.00–14.00, 17.00–01.00 Tues–Fri, 11.00–24.00 Sun Ⓝ Tram: 16 to Molard

Le Rozzel £ ❷   Hobbit-like windows and a tiny terrace add to the appeal of this crêperie in the Old Town, where you can satisfy your pancake cravings with sweet and savoury varieties. ⓐ 18 Grand Rue ☎ 022 312 42 72 🕐 closed Sun Ⓝ Tram: 16 to Molard

Taverne de la Madeleine £ ❸   For local flavour and great-value lunches, make for this centuries-old tavern with creaking beams, exposed stone and the hum of chatter. Homemade fare includes dishes like rösti potatoes and pike-perch filet. ⓐ 20 Rue Toutes-Âmes (off Place de la Madeleine) ☎ 022 310 60 70 🕐 07.30–18.00 Mon–Fri, 09.00–16.30 Sat, closed Sun (Sept–June); 07.30–21.00 Tues–Sat, closed Sun & Mon (July & Aug) Ⓝ Bus: 8, 27 to Place du Port

AFTER DARK

Restaurants

Chez ma Cousine 'on y mange du poulet' £ ❹ Spit-roasted chicken served with mounds of Provençal potatoes is the reason to visit this rustic, good-value restaurant in the centre of town.
ⓐ 6 Place du Bourg-de-Four ⓦ www.chezmacousine.ch
ⓔ info@chezmacousine.ch ⓛ 11.30–23.30 Mon–Sun ⓝ Bus: 3, 5 to Croix-Rouge

Le Morgan £ ❺ Low ceilings and wood panelling give this vaulted cellar a cave-like feel. Take a pew to enjoy classic bistro fare in a warm, friendly setting. ⓐ 14 Rue de la Madeleine
ⓣ 022 311 81 00 ⓛ 11.30–14.30, 17.00–21.00 Mon–Fri, closed Sat & Sun ⓝ Bus: 8, 27 to Place du Port

Au Pied de Cochon ££ ❻ Pig's trotters are the speciality of this ever-popular brasserie oozing turn-of-the-century charm. Service here is snappy and the food delicious. ⓐ 4 Place du Bourg-de-Four ⓣ 022 310 47 97 ⓦ www.pied-de-cochon.ch
ⓛ 06.00–23.00 Mon–Fri, 09.00–23.00 Sat & Sun ⓝ Bus: 3, 5 to Croix-Rouge

Brasserie de l'Hôtel de Ville ££ ❼ There is an old-world feel about this bistro with its polished brass and antique-lined walls. The fare is Swiss with favourites like Geneva-style pork and fondue on the menu. The terrace comes alive in summer.
ⓐ 39 Grand Rue ⓣ 022 311 70 30 ⓔ glosu@bluewin.ch
ⓛ 11.30–23.30 Mon–Sun ⓝ Bus: 3, 5 to Croix-Rouge

Café des Bains ££ ❽   Near the MAMCO, this contemporary
restaurant dishes up poetry on a plate: think sautéed gambas
with prune chutney and polenta or Kerala curry with cumin-
glazed carrots. ⓐ 26 Rue des Bains ❶ 022 321 57 98
Ⓦ www.cafedesbains.com ❶ 11.00–15.00, 18.00–01.00 Tues–Sat,
closed Sun & Mon ❷ Bus: 1 to École-Médecine

Café Papon ££ ❾   Dine beneath the vaults at this chic
restaurant near the Parc des Bastions. Foodies come to mingle
and enjoy tender veal and morels in cream sauce and a nice
glass of wine. ⓐ 1 Rue Henri-Fazy ❶ 022 311 54 28 ❶ 07.00–23.00
Mon–Fri, 09.30–23.00 Sat, closed Sun ❷ Bus: 3, 5 to Croix-Rouge

Senso ££ ❿   Clean lines, muted tones and brown leather create
an ultra-modern setting in which to feast on Italian fusion
cuisine. Olive trees provide shade in the inner courtyard.
ⓐ 56 Rue du Rhône ❶ 022 310 39 90 Ⓦ www.senso-living.ch
❶ 12.00–15.00, 17.00–02.00 Mon–Sat, closed Sun ❶ Bus: 29 to
Molard

Bars & clubs
BBM Wine Bar A red cow welcomes you to this great little wine
bar. Decked out with funky light bulbs and black leather walls, it
also has a terrace with lake views and is great for an aperitif.
ⓐ 12 Quai Général-Guisan ❶ 022 310 92 36
ⓔ bbmwinebar@hotmail.com ❶ 12.00–15.00, 17.00–02.00
Mon–Sat, closed Sun ❷ Bus: 1, 10 to Bel-Air

B Club Bright young things dress up to the nines and head for
this über-cool club to dance till the sun rises. You may well be

sharing the dance floor with celebrities... 12 Place de la Fusterie ☎ 022 311 05 55 ⓦ www.lebaroque.ch ⏰ 23.00–05.00 Mon–Sat, closed Sun ⓝ Bus: 1, 10 to Bel-Air

Café Cuba Latino grooves and salsa moves make this a top after-dark choice. The crowd is hip, the vibe chilled and the caipirinhas flow freely. ⓐ 3 Place du Cirque ☎ 022 328 42 60 ⏰ 07.00–01.00 Mon–Thur, 07.00–02.00 Fri & Sat, 17.00–01.00 Sun ⓝ Tram: 15 to Cirque

Cirkus Bar This new Plainpalais venture is the brainchild of owner Mr Filipowski (who often arrives on rollerblades!). Mellow music, sculpted lights and oriental touches create a Zen-inspired atmosphere in which to enjoy a Manhattan and nibble on fresh Thai finger food. ⓐ 1 Rue Bovy-Lysberg ☎ 022 533 03 20 ⓦ www.cirkusbar.com ⓔ info@cirkusbar.com ⏰ 11.30–01.00 Mon–Thur, 11.30–02.00 Fri, 17.00–02.00 Sat, closed Sun ⓝ Tram: 15 to Cirque

Demi Lune Café Fashionable but understated, candles flicker and mellow grooves play at this cosy bar, where you can sink into a sofa and munch tapas with your cocktail. ⓐ 3 Rue Etienne-Dumont ☎ 022 312 12 90 ⓦ www.demilune.ch ⓔ info@demilune.ch ⏰ 08.45–01.00 Mon–Wed, 08.45–02.00 Thur & Fri, 16.00–02.00 Sat, 16.00–01.00 Sun ⓝ Bus: 3, 5 to Croix-Rouge

L'Ethno Bar Go boho in this arty bar and gallery with high ceilings, wood floors and pillar-box red walls. Everyone who's anyone comes here: students to write, musicians to compose and eco-warriors to plot how to save the world. By night, the ambience is upbeat. ⓐ 1 Rue Bovy-Lysberg ⓣ 023 310 25 21 ⓛ 07.00–02.00 Mon–Fri, 10.00–02.00 Sat & Sun ⓝ Tram: 15 to Cirque

7ème Ciel With moody lighting and sleek contours, this relaxed lounge bar draws trendy urbanites that come to sip mojitos as DJs spin oriental and house tunes. The décor and people are beautiful. ⓐ 7 Rue de la Corraterie ⓣ 022 810 12 40 ⓛ 17.00–02.00 Mon–Sat, closed Sun ⓝ Bus: 3 to Bovy-Lysberg

Spring Brothers A laid-back pub in the centre of town with Guinness on tap and big-screen sports. ⓐ 23 Grand Rue ⓣ 022 312 40 08 ⓛ 17.00–02.00 Mon–Sun ⓝ Bus: 3, 5 to Place Neuve

L'Usine Urban beats pump out from this trendy venue for alternative arts, housed in a former factory. The superb line-up moves from concerts to cutting-edge plays, films and club nights. ⓐ 4 Place des Volontaires ⓣ 022 781 34 90 ⓦ www.usine.ch ⓛ 12.00–15.00, 17.00–02.00 Mon–Sat, closed Sun ⓝ Bus: 10 to Palladium

Right Bank

Five-star hotels punctuating the Quai du Mont-Blanc, crystalline high-rises around the Palace of Nations, boho chic in multicultural Pâquis and gardens hugging the banks of Lake Geneva – the Right Bank has all of this and more. Whether you're seeking the best views of snow-white Mont Blanc, the shade of giant sequoias, a soak in a luxury spa or a mean Thai curry, this district can provide it.

The beauty of the Right Bank lies in its contradictions: from politicians on UN business to Brazilian bartenders in the up-and-coming Pâquis, all-night partying in the Platinum Glam Club to the peace of Mon Repos park.

SIGHTS & ATTRACTIONS

Bains des Pâquis
With seagulls soaring above, waves lapping against the shore and a lighthouse, this pier in central Geneva wouldn't look out of place at the seaside. This wooden boardwalk is where locals gather for a stroll, coffee or picnic – from sharply dressed business people to students relaxing on the rocks. If you're seeking Geneva's hip side, look no further. It also has beaches from which you can swim – even in winter if you want to give the plucky Genevans a run for their money. There's also a sauna and *hammam* where you can warm up after the big chill.
ⓐ 30 Quai du Mont-Blanc ⓣ 022 732 29 74
ⓦ www.bains-des-paquis.ch ⓛ 10.00–21.30 Mon–Sun ⓝ Bus: 1 to Pâquis

Brunswick Monument

The architectural equivalent of a wedding cake, this ornate pink-and-white monument is a riot of skinny spires and stone latticework. Frivolous but fun, the mausoleum is the final resting place of eccentric Duke Charles II of Brunswick, who left his entire fortune to Geneva.

ⓐ Quai du Mont-Blanc ⓝ Bus: 1 to Monthoux

Jardin Botanique (Botanical Gardens)

You can spend an entire afternoon roaming the city's botanical gardens, which fringe the banks of Lake Geneva. The vast green space features an arboretum, Mediterranean greenhouse and gardens nurturing herbs, vegetables, vines, medicinal plants, magnolias and rhododendrons. There are hands-on displays

ⓞ The lighthouse at Bains des Pâquis

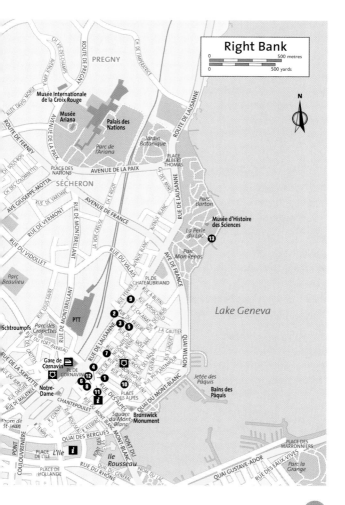

Right Bank

0   500 metres
0   500 yards

N

PREGNY

Musée Internationale de la Croix Rouge
Musée Ariana
Palais des Nations
Jardin Botanique
Parc de l'Ariana

SÉCHERON

Lake Geneva

Musée d'Histoire des Sciences
La Perle du Lac
Parc Mon Repos
Parc Barton

Parc Beaulieu

Schtroumpfs
Parc des Cropettes
PTT

Gare de Cornavin

Notre-Dame

Jetée des Pâquis
Bains des Pâquis

Brunswick Monument
Square du Mont-Blanc

Prom de St-Jean

L'Ile

Ile Rousseau

PLACE DES MARRONNIERS
Parc la Grange

where it's possible to trace the life cycle of a tree and touch different kinds of bark. As well as plant life, the gardens are home to parrots, pink flamingos, wild goats and deer.
@ 1 Chemin de l'Impératrice ⓣ 022 418 51 00 ⓦ www.ville-ge.ch
ⓛ 08.00–19.30 (Apr–Sept); 09.30–17.00 (Oct–Mar) ⓝ Bus: 1, 11, 28 to Jardin Botanique

La Perle du Lac

With its pretty perennials, mature trees and dancing fountains, this lakefront park is one of Geneva's most scenic spots in which to relax and soak up the views. A web of paths takes in statues and clipped box hedges. In summer, the lawn is a sea of brightly coloured dahlias. The park is particularly beautiful in late afternoon when a diffused light turns the Alps various shades of pink.
@ 128 Rue de Lausanne ⓝ Bus: 1 to Sécheron

Palais des Nations (Palace of Nations)

The immense Palace of Nations is the European headquarters of the United Nations. Colourful flags line the avenue leading up to the huge building. It's worth taking a behind-the-scenes tour to glimpse some of the cavernous halls where the political action takes place. The gardens showcase the symbolic Armillary Sphere and the enormous *Broken Chair* sculpture, a protest against landmines.
@ 14 Avenue de la Paix ⓣ 022 917 48 96 ⓦ www.unog.ch
ⓛ 10.00–12.00, 14.00–16.00 Mon–Sun (Apr–Oct); 10.00–17.00 (Nov–Mar) ⓝ Tram: 13 to Nations

Parc Barton

This English-style landscaped garden is dominated by the pink Villa Barton, which Sir Robert Peel acquired in the 19th century. He planted the forest of giant sequoia trees that still stands tall today.

🅐 118 Rue de Lausanne 🅝 Bus: 1 to Sécheron

Parc Mon Repos

Centred around a stately 19th-century villa (Casanova is reputed to have stayed in an earlier house on the site), this attractive lakefront park is a pleasant place to walk through. Enjoy the lush Mediterranean gardens, admire snow-capped Mont Blanc and rest in the shade of ancient trees.

🅐 Rue de Lausanne 🅝 Bus: 1 to Sécheron

🔺 *A monument to cooperation: the Palais des Nations*

Schtroumpfs (Smurfs)

While you're unlikely to see any little blue creatures here, this Gaudíesque building named after the Smurfs does indeed look as though it has stepped straight out of a comic strip. Irregular contours, wacky mosaic designs, wave-shaped balconies and larger-than-life mushrooms define this fantastical edifice in Les Grottes. The unconventional icon is one of Geneva's true hidden gems.

ⓐ 23–29 Rue Louis-Favre Ⓝ Bus: 8 to Grottes

CULTURE

Musée Ariana (Ariana Museum)

Adorned with bas-reliefs and overlooking a beautiful fountain, this museum's pastel pink façade is wonderfully over the top – visit after dark to see it illuminated. The domed neoclassical building shelters an exquisite collection of ceramics and glasswork spanning seven centuries.

ⓐ 10 Avenue de la Paix ❶ 022 418 54 50 ⓔ ariana@ville-ge.ch
🕐 10.00–17.00 Wed–Mon, closed Tues Ⓝ Bus: 8 to Appia. Admission charge

Musée d'Histoire des Sciences (History of Science Museum)

It doesn't cost anything to unravel the wonders of science at this neoclassical mansion set in Perle du Lac park, where you can test out a range of inventions from telescopes and sundials to parabolic mirrors and microscopes.

ⓐ Villa Bartholini, 128 Rue de Lausanne ❶ 022 418 50 60
🕐 10.00–17.00 Wed–Mon, closed Tues Ⓝ Bus: 1 to Sécheron

**Musée Internationale de la Croix Rouge
(International Red Cross Museum)**

Located opposite the Palace of Nations, this fascinating
museum traces the progress of the Red Cross since its
foundation in 1863. Multimedia displays take an in-depth look at
the world's largest humanitarian network, with themes moving
from the 'Written Word', dealing with respect for life, to 'Acts of
Mercy', focusing on Florence Nightingale's benevolent deeds.
Perhaps most poignant of all is the 'Wall of Time', charting
epidemics, tragedies and armed conflicts.

ⓐ 17 Avenue de la Paix ⓣ 022 748 95 25 ⓦ www.micr.ch
ⓛ 10.00–17.00 Wed–Mon, closed Tues ⓝ Tram: 13 to Nations.
Admission charge

🔺 *The beautiful Villa Bartholoni, home to the Musée d'Histoire des Sciences*

RETAIL THERAPY

Manor An ideal one-stop shop close to the station, this six-level department store is the biggest in Geneva and stocks women's fashion, fragrances, sportswear, home design, jewellery and lingerie. The top floor affords panoramic views from the terrace. ⓐ 6 Rue de Cornavin ⓣ 022 909 46 99 ⓦ www.manor.ch ⓛ 09.00–19.00 Mon–Wed, 09.00–21.00 Thur, 09.00–19.30 Fri, 08.30–18.00 Sat, closed Sun ⓝ Tram: 13 to Cornavin

Metro Shopping Cornavin This mall near the station is home to a clutch of high-street stores including Yves Rocher, Swarovski, Lacoste and Merkur for Swiss chocolate. There's also a tea room, bakery, sushi bar and newsagent. ⓐ 10 Place de Cornavin ⓣ 022 900 22 10 ⓦ www.metroshopping.ch ⓛ 09.00–19.00 Mon–Fri, 09.00–17.00 Sat, closed Sun ⓝ Tram: 13 to Cornavin

SCINTILLATING SPA

If you fancy a little pampering, head for La Réserve spa. Ranked one of the top retreats in the world, this temple of self-indulgence overlooking Lake Geneva is the playground of celebrities. Signature treatments include balneotherapy, ayurvedic massage and the three-hour 'Swiss bliss' package. It's exclusive and expensive, but the feel-good factor is worthy of the 5 stars. ⓐ 301 Route de Lausanne ⓣ 022 959 59 99 ⓦ www.lareserve.ch ⓛ 08.30–20.00 Mon–Sun ⓛ Train: Les Tuileries

Swatch Shop Visit this brightly coloured store for the latest Swatch watches in all shapes and sizes.

ⓐ 19 Rue du Mont-Blanc ⓣ 022 900 22 10 🕒 09.00–19.00 Mon–Fri, 09.00–18.00 Sat, closed Sun Ⓝ Bus: 8 to Mont-Blanc

TAKING A BREAK

Boky £ ❶ Chefs whip up tasty and cheap Japanese, Chinese and Malay specialities at this no-frills restaurant. ⓐ 21 Rue des Alpes ⓣ 022 738 37 94 🕒 11.00–02.00 Mon–Sun Ⓝ Bus: 1 to Alpes

Da Antonio £ ❷ Authentic wood-fired Neapolitan pizza is the main reason to visit this terracotta-tiled restaurant. ⓐ 52 Rue de Lausanne ⓣ 022 738 70 78 Ⓝ Tram: 13, 15 to Môle

Maison de l'Ancre £ ❸ If you're on a tight budget, this relaxed hospice café serves the cheapest lunch in town – from fresh salads and sandwiches to homemade cakes and coffee.
ⓐ 34 Rue de Lausanne ⓣ 022 420 58 00 🕒 08.00–22.15 Mon–Thur, 08.00–23.15 Fri, closed Sat & Sun Ⓝ Tram: 13, 15 to Môle

Il Monte Bianco £ ❹ Crammed with the finest Italian fare, from whole hams to wines and olives, the lunchtime queue speaks volumes for the quality. ⓐ 9 Rue Chaponnière ⓣ 022 732 41 54 🕒 08.00–20.00 Mon–Fri, closed Sat & Sun Ⓝ Tram: 13, 15 to Môle

Só Mel £ ❺ Locals enjoy yummy Portuguese pastries at this unpretentious tea room. ⓐ 52 Rue de Lausanne ⓣ 022 732 34 58 🕒 06.00–19.00 Thur–Tues, closed Wed Ⓝ Tram: 13, 15 to Môle

AFTER DARK

Restaurants

Café de Paris £ ❻ Vegetarians beware! There's only one thing on the menu at this classic French bistro – steak served with fries. It can be a bit of a squeeze to get in, but the buzz adds to the atmosphere. ⓐ 26 Rue du Mont-Blanc ❶ 022 732 84 50 ⓦ www.cafe-de-paris.ch ⏱ 11.00–23.00 Mon–Sun ⓝ Bus: 8 to Mont-Blanc

Café Gandhi £ ❼ Decorated with red velvet, wood carvings and fairy lights, this unassuming restaurant serves tasty fish curries and dhal with fluffy nan breads. ⓐ 37 Rue de Neuchâtel ❶ 022 731 61 61 ⓦ www.gandhi.ch ⏱ 12.00–14.30, 19.00–23.00 Mon–Sat, 12.00–14.30 Sun ⓝ Bus: 1 to Monthoux

Restaurant Mañana £ ❽ Feisty fajitas, vegetarian enchiladas and free-flowing tequila are on the menu at this Mexican-inspired restaurant above the Cactus Club. ⓐ 3 Rue Chaponnière ❶ 022 732 21 31 ⏱ 12.00–14.00, 18.00–23.30 Mon–Sat, 18.00–23.30 Sun ⓝ Bus: 8 to Mont-Blanc

Ze do Pipo £ ❾ Tuck into *bacalhau assado* (baked cod) at this inviting little restaurant dishing up authentic Portuguese specialities. ⓐ 57 Rue de Lausanne ❶ 022 738 88 21 ⏱ 08.00–23.30 Mon–Sat, closed Sun ⓝ Tram: 13, 15 to Môle

Bistrot du Boeuf Rouge ££ ❿ In the heart of the trendy Pâquis district, this bistro is a blast from the past. The menu specialises in Lyonnaise fare such as *andouillette beaujolaise* (tripe sausage) and *boudin noir* (blood sausage). ❸ 17 Rue Alfred-Vincent ❶ 022 732 75 37 Ⓦ www.boeufrouge.ch ❶ Mon–Fri Ⓝ Bus: 1 to Monthoux

La Matze ££ ⓫   This rustic restaurant evokes a snug alpine chalet. Savour hearty fare like cheese fondue or beef charbonnade. ❸ 7 Rue Chaponnière ❶ 022 732 79 61 Ⓦ www.la-matze.ch ❶ 12.00–14.00, 19.00–23.00 Mon–Fri, 19.00–23.00 Sat, closed Sun Ⓝ Bus: 8 to Mont-Blanc

El Mektoub ££ ⓬   You'd be forgiven for thinking you were in Marrakech at this Aladdin's cave of a restaurant. Sample North African favourites like couscous and tender lamb with artichokes. ❸ 5 Rue Chaponnière ❶ 022 738 70 31 Ⓦ www.elmektoub.com ❶ 12.00–24.00 Mon–Fri, 18.00–24.00 Sat, closed Sun Ⓝ Bus: 8 to Mont-Blanc

La Perle du Lac £££ ⓭   The views from this stylish restaurant are as delightful as the gourmet menu. ❸ Parc Mon Repos ❶ 022 909 10 20 Ⓦ www.laperledulac.ch ❷ info@laperledulac.ch ❶ 11.00–01.00 Mon–Sun Ⓝ Bus: 1 to Sécheron

Bars
Cactus Club The cocktails at this underground bar take some beating. Bursting with young partygoers at the weekends, this is the place to dance the night away to soulful sounds. ❸ 3 Rue Chaponnière ❶ 022 732 21 31 ❶ 18.00–01.00 Sun–Thur, 18.00–02.00 Fri & Sat Ⓝ Bus: 8 to Mont-Blanc

Lord Jim This cheery British pub has some decent beers on tap and is a cosy spot to catch sports on the big screen. 32 Rue de Lausanne 022 732 52 92 www.lordjimpub.ch 17.00–02.00 Mon–Fri, 18.00–02.00 Sat & Sun Tram: 13 to Môle

Mr Pickwick Pub This cosy English pub claims to be Switzerland's oldest. Expect the works – from 13 beers on tap to big-screen sports, live bands, karaoke and quiz nights. 80 Rue de Lausanne 022 731 67 97 www.mrpickwick.ch info@mrpickwick.ch 10.00–02.00 Mon–Sun Tram: 13 to Butini

New York Bar Doubling as a restaurant, this elegant bar exudes old-world charm. You can spend a leisurely evening here sipping a bourbon or malt whisky. 24 Rue du Cendrier 022 731 76 98 07.00–02.00 Mon–Sat, closed Sun Bus: 29 to Chantepoulet

Platinum Glam Club If you're painting the Right Bank red, you'll probably wind up at this ultra-hip club where, after persuading the doormen to let you in, you'll enjoy Geneva's wildest parties. 18 Quai du Seujet 022 738 90 91 www.platinum-club.ch 23.00–05.00 Mon–Sun Tram: 16 to Isaac-Mercier

Willi's This upbeat lounge bar is the place to see and be seen on the fashionable Rue du Mont-Blanc. The terrace is perfect for people watching. 11 Rue du Mont-Blanc 022 732 77 09 willis@arthurs.ch 07.00–02.00 Mon–Fri, 08.00–02.00 Sat, 09.00–02.00 Sun Bus: 8 to Mont-Blanc

Carouge

Although just a 15-minute tram ride south of the centre, Carouge feels a world apart from Geneva. It was barely a speck on the map until 1754 when it became part of the Kingdom of Sardinia and King Victor Amédée III transformed the tiny hamlet into a flourishing town. The Piedmont landmarks that sprang up in the 18th century give the town its distinctly Italian atmosphere.

The beauty of Carouge lies in its understated charm and laid-back feel. While its sights might not quite rival those of other districts in Geneva, its sunny squares, pavement cafés and green-shuttered houses festooned with flower baskets ensure that it captivates nevertheless. You can easily spend a day here boutique shopping, strolling the banks of the River Arve and soaking up the local flavour in bohemian cafés. This little taste of Sardinia is still off the beaten tourist track, so discover it soon.

SIGHTS & ATTRACTIONS

Église Ste-Croix (St Cross Church)

This baroque cruciform church has a striking façade with slender columns, a central tower and Piedmontese elements – glance up to see the cockerel perching on the cross. An oasis of calm, the interior features grey-and-white frescoes, two rose windows and an organ dating from the romantic period. But the church's greatest claim to fame is that it houses Switzerland's largest carillon, comprising 36 bells, which you're likely to hear before you see.

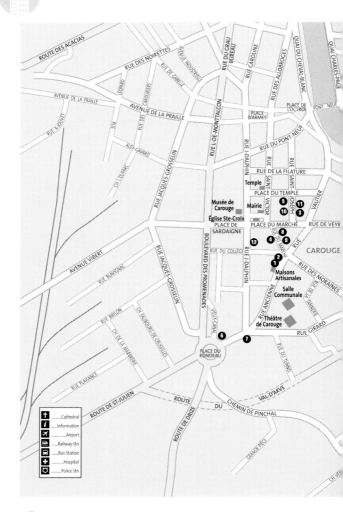

ROUTE DES ACACIAS
RUE DES NOIRETTES
RUE DE CARELLE
AVENUE INDUSTRIELLE
RUE DU GRAU BUREAU
RUE CAROLINE
RUE DES ALLOBROGES
QUAI DU CHEVAL-BLANC
QUAI CHARLES-PAGE
PONT-NEUF
PLACE DE L'OCTROI
AVENUE DE LA PRAILLE
LEOPARD
RUE DES CAROUBIERS
PLACE D'ARMES
RUE DU PONT NEUF
AVENUE DE LA PRAILLE
RUE DES
RUE J.-L-DE-MONTFALCON
RUE J.-DALPHIN
RUE SAINT
RUE DE LA FILATURE
ALEX-GAVARD
RUE A.-JOLIVET
CH. COLLABAC
RUE JACQUES-GROSSELIN
Temple
SAINT
Musée de Carouge
PLACE DU TEMPLE
RUE VICTOR
Mairie
JOSEPH
RUE VAUTIER
Église Ste-Croix
PLACE DE SARDAIGNE
PLACE DU MARCHÉ
RUE DE VEYR
RUE DU COLLÈGE
CAROUGE
AVENUE VIBERT
BOULEVARD DES PROMENADES
RUE J.-DALPHIN
RUE ANCIENNE
RUE ST.-JEANNE
RUE DES MORAINES
RUE BLAVIGNAC
RUE JACQUES-GROSSELIN
Maisons Artisanales
RUE BAYLON
VIEUX CANAL
Salle Communale
CH. FAUBOURG-DE-CRUSEILLES
Théâtre de Carouge
RUE GIRARD
CH. DE LA MARBRERIE
RUE DU TUNNEL
PLACE DU RONDEAU
RUE PLAISANCE
ROUTE DE ST-JULIEN
ROUTE DE DRIZE
ROUTE DU
CHEMIN DE PINCHAL
VAL-D'ARVE
GRANDE-PIÈCE
CH. VE

Cathedral
Information
Airport
Railway Stn
Bus Station
Hospital
Police Stn

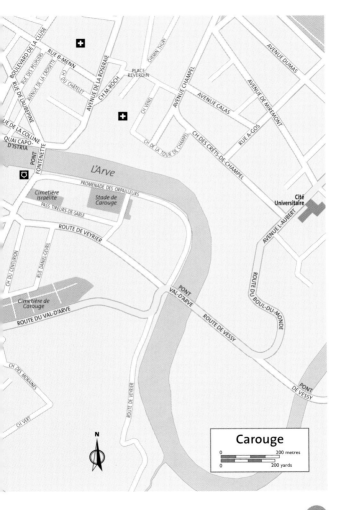

BOULEVARD DE LA CLUSE
RUE DES PEUPLIERS
RUE DE L'AUBÉPINE
AVENUE DE LA GROSETTE
RUE B.-MENN
DU CHÂTELET
AVENUE DE LA ROSERAIE
CH. M.-ROCH
PLACE REVERDIN
CHEMIN THURY
CH. VERET
AVENUE CHAMPEL
AVENUE CALAS
AVENUE DUMAS
AVENUE DE MIREMONT
RUE DE LA COLLINE
QUAI CAPO D'ISTRIA
PONT FONTENETTE
CH. DE LA TOUR DE CHAMPEL
CH. DES CRÊTS-DE-CHAMPEL
RUE A.-GOS
L'Arve
PROMENADE DES ORPAILLEURS
Cimetière Israélite
Stade de Carouge
PASS. TIREURS-DE-SABLE
ROUTE DE VEYRIER
Cité Universitaire
AVENUE L.-AUBERT
CH. DU CENTURION
RUE DANIEL GEVRIL
Cimetière de Carouge
ROUTE DU VAL-D'ARVE
PONT VAL-D'ARVE
ROUTE DE VESSY
ROUTE DU BOUL-DU-MONDE
CH. DES MORAINES
ROUTE DE VEYRIER
PONT DE VESSY
CH. VERT

N

Carouge
0   200 metres
0   200 yards

ⓐ Place du Marché ⓣ 022 342 26 84 ⓦ www.saintecroix.ch
ⓛ 09.00–18.30 Mon–Sun ⓝ Tram: 12, 13 to Marché

Mairie (Town Hall)
Squatting in the shadow of the church, the town hall is the
brainchild of Italian architect Giuseppe Piacenza. The sandy-
coloured structure was built in 1777 as a presbytery and today it
proudly flies the Carouge flag (a white lion beside a tree set
against a red background).
ⓐ 14 Place du Marché ⓦ www.carouge.ch ⓝ Tram: 12, 13 to Marché

ⓢ *The elegant Église Ste-Croix*

Maisons Artisanales (Craftsmen's Houses)

Once home to the town's craftsmen, these Mediterranean-inspired houses are some of the best-preserved examples of 18th-century architecture in Carouge. Take a peek at their twisting staircases, arcades and leafy inner courtyards.

🅐 8–30 Rue Ancienne Ⓝ Tram: 12, 13 to Marché

Place du Marché (Market Square)

The epicentre of Carouge life, this picture-perfect square is fringed with plane trees and overshadowed by the church. Be sure to look at the Blavignac fountain, a tribute to the River Arve shaped from rock and bronze. The twice-weekly market injects life into the square and a string of pavement cafés and restaurants reel in locals and visitors. It's a great spot to enjoy lunch or coffee and indulge in some prime people watching.

🅐 Place du Marché Ⓝ Tram: 12, 13 to Marché

Pont-Neuf

With its trio of limestone arches, this bridge bears an uncanny resemblance to its namesake in Paris. Although the river has washed it away several times in the past, the current bridge dating back to 1817 is built of sterner stuff. From here you can admire the silver-grey waters of the meandering River Arve, a tributary of the Rhône that's fed by alpine glaciers. It's possible to stroll along the river's tree-lined banks and, if you're lucky, spot herons and beavers.

🅐 Pont-Neuf Ⓝ Tram: 12, 13 to Armes

Temple

Quite aptly named temple, this neoclassical church boasts peristyle columns and a Grecian-style pediment. Built in the early 19th century, this gem includes Byzantine-style wood carvings and elaborately frescoed vaults. It is open for guided tours and Sunday morning services only.

ⓐ Place du Temple ⓑ (Guided tours) 08.00–13.00 Wed & Sat
ⓝ Tram: 12, 13 to Marché

◭ Take a tour of the neoclassical Temple

CULTURE

Musée de Carouge (Carouge Museum)

The imposing 18th-century Montanrouge House shelters this intriguing museum, which provides an insight into Carouge life past and present. Alongside temporary exhibitions, the permanent collection features a clutch of ceramics, paintings, art deco crafts and contemporary works by Carouge artists. Be sure to take a look at the Sardinian garden while you're there.

ⓐ 2 Place de Sardaigne ⓣ 022 342 33 83 ⓦ www.carouge.ch ⓛ 14.00–18.00 Tues–Sun, closed Mon ⓝ Tram: 12, 13 to Marché

Théâtre de Carouge (Carouge Theatre)

Experimental productions, cutting-edge plays and perennial favourites take to the stage of Carouge's intimate theatre, which was founded in 1958.

ⓐ 57 Rue Ancienne ⓣ 022 343 43 43 ⓦ www.theatredecarouge-geneve.ch ⓛ 19.00 Tues, Thur & Sat, 20.00 Wed & Fri, 17.00 Sun ⓝ Tram: 13 to Carouge

RETAIL THERAPY

Asaya This dinky boutique is crammed with Indonesian crafts, from multicoloured elephants to intricate woodcarvings.

ⓐ 16 Rue Ancienne ⓣ 022 301 93 60 ⓛ 07.00–14.30 Mon–Fri, 08.45–14.30 Sat, closed Sun ⓝ Tram: 13 to Carouge

Auteur du Bain There is a whiff of nostalgia in this quirky shop, where tin tubs brim with dreamy bath products. Natural ingredients are used to create heart-shaped soaps on sticks and edible-looking bath sweets, cakes, chocolates, puddings and confetti. Lotions and potions scented with Moroccan rose, Egyptian jasmine and amber will make you want to run a bath straight away. ⓐ 12 Rue Saint-Joseph ⓣ 022 300 52 73 ⓛ 10.00–12.30, 14.00–19.00 Tues–Fri, 10.00–19.00 Sat, closed Sun ⓝ Tram: 12, 13 to Marché

Betjeman & Barton The red walls are lined with every type of tea, teapot and cup imaginable at this cha-crazy store. A unique

CRAFTY CAROUGE

Carouge's creative roots stretch back to the 18th century, when the town was home to a plethora of carpenters, cobblers, blacksmiths, dressmakers, tanneries and watchmakers. The arty spirit is still alive and kicking today; the narrow streets a maze of musty antique shops, Lilliputian galleries and boutiques that are full of curiosities, original handicrafts and one-off local designs.

As you amble through the town, you'll come across the workshops and boutiques of potters, glassblowers, ceramicists, jewellers, hatters, fashion designers, *chocolatiers* and confectioners. The beauty of shopping here is that you can often meet the makers themselves, and discover the raw materials and processes that go into their work. If you want high-street names and designer labels, stick to Geneva centre; but if you're seeking arty gifts, it has got to be crafty Carouge.

brew to look out for is *La Dame du Lac*, a blend of Mirabelle plum, strawberry, apple and caramel. You'll also find fresh ginger juice and lavender confiture here. ⓐ 35 Rue Saint-Joseph ⓣ 022 301 20 30 ⓦ www.barton.ch ⓔ info@barton.ch ⓛ 09.45–17.30 Mon–Fri, 09.45–13.00, 14.00–17.00 Sat, closed Sun ⓝ Tram: 12, 13 to Marché

Bignens Vins This intoxicating store offers a staggering choice of regional and world wines. ⓐ 2 Rue du Marché ⓣ 022 301 75 40 ⓦ www.bignens.ch ⓛ 08.30–12.30, 14.00–18.45 Mon–Sat, closed Sun ⓝ Tram: 12, 13 to Marché

Farmers' Market Taking over the main square twice a week, this market serves up voluptuous fruits, bunches of fresh lavender, farm-fresh Reblochon, handmade breads, truffles, homemade preserves and honey. Even if you don't plan to buy, come to soak up the buzzing atmosphere and taste local wines. ⓐ Place du Marché ⓛ 08.00–13.00 Wed & Sat ⓝ Tram: 12, 13 to Marché

Karavan Seray From mosaic vases to leatherwork and intricate woodcarvings, this shop stocks quality crafts from Tunisia, Morocco and Algeria. ⓐ 22 Rue Saint-Joseph ⓣ 022 343 96 11 ⓛ 10.00–18.30 Mon–Fri, 09.30–17.00 Sat, closed Sun ⓝ Tram: 13 to Carouge

Paloma de la Paz Pick up arty gifts like ceramics, tapestries and candles in this boutique. ⓐ 42 Rue Ancienne ⓣ 022 342 61 98 ⓛ 07.00–14.30 Mon–Fri, 08.45–14.30 Sat, closed Sun ⓝ Tram: 13 to Carouge

Philippe Pascoët Master *chocolatier* Philippe Pascoët pours his passion and know-how into creating Carouge's finest chocolates. The cocoa-rich pralines and truffles are infused with herbs like fresh mint, basil, star anis, rosemary, sage and even tobacco. ⓐ 22 Rue Saint-Joseph ⓣ 022 301 20 58 ⓦ www.philippe-pascoet.ch ⓛ 10.00–18.30 Mon–Fri, 09.30–17.00 Sat, closed Sun ⓝ Tram: 12, 13 to Marché

Verrerie Berlin Artisanale It may look like marble or precious stones, but everything in this pocket-sized boutique is handcrafted from glass. ⓐ 4 Rue Saint-Joseph ⓣ 022 343 10 43 ⓛ 15.00–18.30 Tues–Fri, 09.00–12.00 Sat, closed Sun & Mon ⓝ Tram: 12, 13 to Marché

Zabo Hat lovers should visit this kooky boutique and workshop; it has colourful creations from the woolly to the wacky that will make you stand out from the crowd. ⓐ 31 Rue Saint-Joseph ⓣ 022 301 75 76 ⓦ www.zabo.ch ⓛ 14.00–18.30 Tues–Fri, 10.00–12.30, 14.00–17.00 Sat, closed Sun & Mon ⓝ Tram: 12, 13 to Marché

TAKING A BREAK

Café de l'Aigle £ ❶ Shabby chic sums up this convivial café, where the walls are graced with arty shots of India. It's a pleasant spot for a light lunch or drinks with the locals at the bar. ⓐ 42 Rue Ancienne ⓣ 022 342 61 98 ⓛ 07.00–14.30 Mon–Fri, 08.45–14.30 Sat, closed Sun ⓝ Tram: 13 to Carouge

Calm £ ❷   It's easy to see the appeal of this effortlessly cool café: jazzy lounge music, delicious home-grown food and a relaxed vibe that will indeed leave you feeling very calm. Snacks include goat's-cheese quiche, yoghurt cake, warming soups and fresh-pressed juices. With wood beams, flickering candles and squishy leather chairs, the lounge is a great place to hibernate. ⓐ 36 Rue Ancienne ⓣ 022 301 22 20 ⓛ 07.00–14.30 Mon–Fri, 08.45–14.30 Sat, closed Sun ⓝ Tram: 13 to Carouge

Gelato Mania £ ❸   When the weather is warm, the handmade ice cream and sorbets at this hole-in-the-wall gelateria are refreshing. ⓐ 43 Rue Saint-Joseph ⓔ gelatomania@bluewin.ch ⓛ 12.00–23.00 Tues–Thur, 11.00–24.00 Fri–Sun, closed Mon (May–Aug); 12.00–18.00 Tues–Sun, closed Mon (Sept & Oct) ⓝ Tram: 12, 13 to Marché

Martel £ ❹   Avid chocolate lovers should make for this *confiserie* which serves mouth-watering pralines, éclairs, glistening strawberry tarts and bite-sized petits fours. Sample them in the elegant tearoom ⓐ 8 Rue du Marché ⓣ 022 342 00 45 ⓛ 07.30–19.00 Tues–Fri, 07.30–18.00 Sat & Sun ⓝ Tram: 12, 13 to Marché

Wolfisberg £ ❺   The smell of freshly baked bread fills the air at this spacious pâtisserie and tearoom in the centre of town. The design is contemporary with bright colours, and the baguettes and pastries are superb. ⓐ 5 Place du Temple ⓣ 022 342 32 19 ⓛ 06.30–19.00 Thur–Tues, closed Wed ⓝ Tram: 12, 13 to Marché

AFTER DARK

Restaurants

Au Boccalino £ ❻ Red-checked tablecloths, tiled floors and beamed ceilings give this cave-like restaurant the feel of a rustic Italian trattoria. The well-prepared antipasti, wood-fired pizza and fresh salads served with Chianti would make mamma proud. ⓐ 4 Place du Rondeau ❶ 022 343 73 87 ⓔ leboccalino@bluewin.ch ❶ 11.00–14.00, 18.30–23.00 Ⓝ Tram: 13 to Carouge

Au Lion d'Or de Carouge £ ❼ Housed in a 300-year-old building, this unpretentious little restaurant draws locals who come for the flavoursome food and great-value *plat du jour*. Take a seat in the vaulted cellar or in the pretty courtyard to savour a fusion of French and Italian flavours with dishes such as risotto and duck foie gras with cider apples. ⓐ 53 Rue Ancienne ❶ 022 342 18 13 ❶ Mon–Sat, closed Sun Ⓝ Tram: 13 to Carouge

La Bourse £ ❽ At the heart of Carouge, this classic brasserie is all exposed brick, warm wood and soft lighting. Pull up a chair in the frescoed cellar and choose between favourites such as *marmite du pêcheur* (fish casserole), champagne fondue and Bourgogne snails. The prix-fixe menu is chalked up on a blackboard. ⓐ 7 Place du Marché ❶ 022 342 04 66 ❶ 12.00–14.00, 19.00–23.00 Mon–Sat, closed Sun Ⓝ Tram: 12, 13 to Marché

Carlito £ ❾ The menu is predominantly Swiss at this snug wood-panelled bistro next to the church. The number of rösti potato specialities is staggering and the four-cheese fondue comes recommended. ⓐ 7 Rue du Marché ⓣ 022 300 26 56 ⓛ 11.00–14.00, 18.00–22.00 Mon–Sun Ⓝ Tram: 12, 13 to Marché

La Cave £ ⓾ The walls are lined with gleaming wine bottles at this snug enclave, where fondue burners glow on the tables. With specialities like tomato fondue and meringues with Gruyère cream there's no point counting the calories here. ⓐ 42 Rue Saint-Joseph ⓣ 022 300 50 06 ⓛ 18.00–23.00 Mon–Sat, closed Sun Ⓝ Tram: 12, 13 to Marché

Épiaprès £ ⓫ Mediterranean touches and fusion cuisine are the big draw here. After dark, the inviting café transforms into a vibrant restaurant serving tasty Spanish tapas and waistline-expanding Swiss treats such as chocolate fondue with fresh fruit. ⓐ 37 Rue Saint-Joseph ⓣ 022 342 03 32 ⓦ www.epiapres.ch ⓛ 06.00–24.00 Mon–Fri, 10.00–24.00 Sat, closed Sun Ⓝ Tram: 12, 13 to Marché

La Table ££ ⓬ Serious foodies are in for a treat at this stylish, light-filled restaurant close to the main square. It may look unassuming from outside, but it's the kitchen that counts. Dishes like curried salmon and tender lamb with ratatouille keep people coming back for more. ⓐ 31 Rue Jacques-Dalphin ⓣ 022 301 13 22 ⓛ 16.00–02.00 Mon–Sat, closed Sun Ⓝ Tram: 12, 13 to Marché

Bars & clubs
Le Chat Noir If you want to get your claws into Carouge's after-dark scene, head for the black cat. Staging some of Geneva's

hottest live music, the cellar of this hip venue rocks with everything from jazz to rock concerts, chanson and operetta. DJs on the decks keep the tiny dance floor crammed until the early hours of the morning. ⓐ 13 Rue Vautier ⓣ 022 343 49 98 ⓦ www.chatnoir.ch ⓔ chatnoir@chatnoir.ch ⓛ 18.00–04.00 Mon–Thur, 18.00–05.00 Fri & Sat, closed Sun ⓝ Tram: 12, 13 to Marché

L'Imprévu Black leather chairs, wood floors and original art make this a laid-back spot in which to enjoy a cappuccino by day or cocktail by night – try a Mojito or Cuba Libre. ⓐ 37–39 Rue Vautier ⓣ 022 343 77 00 ⓦ www.imprevu.ch ⓛ 08.00–01.00 Mon–Fri, 08.00–02.00 Sat, closed Sun ⓝ Tram: 12, 13 to Marché

Lion Rouge Pub This good old-fashioned pub is as far removed from 'posh' Geneva as they come. The cosy den is kitted out with a red telephone box and offers an arm-long list of beers including Amstel, Kilkenny and Erdinger. ⓐ 2 Rue de Veyrier ⓣ 022 343 55 07 ⓛ 16.00–02.00 Mon–Sat, closed Sun ⓝ Tram: 12, 13 to Marché

Qu'importe Inspired by Alfred de Musset's phrase, '*Qu'importe le flacon…*', this funky lounge bar is a popular spot. Sink into the chocolate-hued leather sofas to unwind with a glass of wine and tapas by the fire. The terrace hums with life in summer. ⓐ 1 Rue Ancienne ⓣ 022 342 15 25 ⓔ contact@quimporte.ch ⓛ 08.00–01.00 Tues–Thur, 08.00–02.00 Fri & Sat, closed Sun & Mon ⓝ Tram: 12, 13 to Ancienne

▶ *Boats and battlements at Annecy*

Lausanne

Capital of the canton of Vaud, Lausanne is an effervescent university city that boasts pristine Belle Époque architecture, a hilltop medieval Old Town and a glut of vibrant bars that buzz by night.

GETTING THERE

The A1 motorway links Geneva to Lausanne and the journey takes 40 minutes by car. The city is also easy to reach by public transport, with SBB trains departing frequently from Geneva's main station with a journey time of approximately 45 minutes. In summer, a pleasant way to arrive is by ferry – contact CGN for further details. Ⓦ www.cgn.ch

SIGHTS & ATTRACTIONS

Cathédrale de Notre-Dame (Notre-Dame Cathedral)

Lausanne's Gothic cathedral looms large above the Old Town. Inside, light pierces the 13th-century rose window and imbues the interior with a sense of calm. For sweeping views over the city's rooftops, head for the terrace.
ⓐ Place de la Cathédrale ⓣ 021 316 71 61 ⓛ 07.00–19.00 Mon–Fri, 08.00–19.00 Sat & Sun Ⓝ Bus: 16 to Pierre-Viret

Château Saint-Maire (Saint-Maire Castle)

The spires of this 14th-century red-brick castle are like something out of a classic fairy tale. One-time home of bishops

and Bernese bailiffs, it is now the seat of the cantonal
government. The terrace affords far-reaching views over the city.
ⓐ Place du Château ⓣ 022 342 26 84 Ⓝ Bus: 16 to Pierre-Viret

Hôtel de Ville (Town Hall)

The epicentre of Lausanne's Old Town, this arcaded Renaissance
building overlooks the Fountain of Justice – get there on the
hour to see historical figurines parade from the clock on the
wall behind.
ⓐ Place de la Palud ⓣ 022 342 26 84 Ⓝ Bus: 16 to Pierre-Viret

🔺 *Parade on the promenade at Ouchy*

Geneva region

0   10 km
0   5 miles

La Chaux-du-Dombief
Pont-de-Poitte
Clairvaux-les-Lacs
Orgelet
JURA
Varennes-St-Sauveur
Cuiseaux
Chambéria
Charchilla
Bienne
Lac de Vouglans
A39
St-Amour
St-Julien
Arinthod
St-Claude
Coligny
Septmoncel
St-Étienne-du-Bois
Dortan
Les Bouchoux
Viry
Crêt de la Neige 1718 ▲
Treffort-Cuisiat
Thoirette
Suran
Ain
Viriat
Izernore
Oyonnax
Semine
Bourg-en-Bresse
A404
Mont Burdet 1043
FRANCE
Péron
Cevzériat
Le Grand Crêt d'Eau 1621 ▲
St-Martin-du-Frêne
Nantua
Valserine
Lent
A40
St-Martin-du-Mont
Châtillon-en-Michaille
Collonges
AIN
Oignin
Bellegarde-sur-Valserine
A40
Ponein
Crêt des Éculaz 1014 ▲
Brénod
Crêt du Nu 1351
Rhône
Châtillon-la-Palud
Ambronay
Ruffieu
Frangy
A42
Jujurieux
Albarine
Bassy
Lyon
Germany
St-Rambert-en-Bugey
Seyssel
Thusy
France
Switzerland
Fur
Geneva region
Italy
Crêt de Pont 1059 ▲
Champagne-en-Valromey
Grand Colombier 1531
Rumilly
Serran
Cluse des Hôpitaux
Villebois
Artemare
Ruffieux

Le Sentier
Vallée de Joux
Mont Tendre
1679
Cossonay
SWITZERLAND
A1
Epalignes
Bois-d'Amont
VAUD
Bière
Renens
LAUSANNE
Morges
A9
Les Rousses
Ouchy
Cully
Rolle
St-Prex
La Dôle
1677
St-Cergue
A1
Lake Geneva
Nyon
Yvoire
Lugrin
Divonne-les-Bains
Evian-les-Bains
Meillerie
Thonon-les-Bains
Gex
Sciez
Vacheresse
Versoix
Douvaine
Allinges
Ferney-Voltaire
Geneva Airport
Brevon
Vernier
Ville-la-Grand
Bons-en-Chablais
Le Biot
Abondance
GENEVA
Boëge
Montriond
Lancy
Annemasse
Risse
Roc d'Enfer
2244
Avoriaz
Carouge
Veyrier
Faucigny
Mieussy
Les Gets
St-Julien-en-Genevois
Arve
A40
Le Môle
1863
Taninges
La-Roche-sur-Foron
Bonneville
Marignier
Giffre
Genevois
Thyez
N
Salève
Cruseilles
A41
Scionzier
Cluses
Choisy
Thorens-Glières
Borne
Magland
Flaine
A41
HAUTE SAVOIE
Borée
A40
Cran-Gevrier
Annecy-le-Vieux
La St-Jean-de-Sixt
Pointe Percée
2752
Sévrier
Lake Annecy
Annecy
Thônes
Fier
Sallanches
Megève

	City
	Large Town
	Small Town
	Motorway
	Main Road
	Minor Road
	Airport
	Railway

Jardin Botanique (Botanical Gardens)

Steep paths weave through these hilltop botanical gardens, which are home to 6,000 species, including medicinal, alpine and tropical plants. From the top there are 360° views over Lausanne and the lake.

ⓐ Avenue de Beauregard ⓣ 021 316 99 88
ⓦ www.botanique.vd.ch ⓛ 10.00–17.30 Mon–Sun (Mar–Oct); closed Nov–Feb ⓝ Bus: 1 to Beauregard

Ouchy

The port of Ouchy is a far cry from the city's bustle: the waterfront promenade is where the locals come to relax, stroll and drink in views of the Alps. Fringed with flower-strewn gardens, the quays are home to grand hotels, smart restaurants, the Olympic Park and a castle. Boats bobbing in the marina, candyfloss sellers, carousels and street entertainers give it a seaside feel.

ⓐ Quai d'Ouchy ⓝ Bus: 2 to Navigation

CULTURE

Fondation de l'Hermitage

Situated in the Bois de Sauvabelin park, this pink 19th-century residence houses an exceptional permanent collection featuring works by Degas, Sisley and Magritte. The gallery frequently hosts temporary exhibitions.

ⓐ 2 Route du Signal ⓣ 021 320 50 01
ⓦ www.fondation-hermitage.ch ⓔ info@fondation-hermitage.ch
ⓛ 11.00–18.00 Tues–Sun, closed Mon ⓝ Bus: 3 to Motte. Admission charge

Musée Historique (History Museum)

This intriguing museum opposite the cathedral traces Lausanne's history from the Ice Age to the 20th century. Low-beamed rooms and narrow passageways are the backdrop for chronological displays that include Neolithic skeletons, religious iconography, silverware and antique musical instruments.

ⓐ 4 Place de la Cathédrale ⓣ 021 315 41 01

ⓦ www.lausanne.ch/mhl ⓛ 11.00–18.00 Tues–Thur, 11.00–17.00 Fri–Sun, closed Mon ⓝ Bus: 16 to Pierre-Viret. Admission charge

Musée Olympique (Olympic Museum)

Shaped from marble and soaring above the Olympic Park on Ouchy embankment, this monumental building is a tribute to Lausanne's Olympic heritage – the city has been home to the International Olympic Committee (IOC) since 1915. Themed displays cover all aspects of the Games.

ⓐ Quai d'Ouchy ⓣ 021 621 65 11 ⓦ www.olympic.org

ⓛ 09.00–18.00 Mon–Sun (Apr–Oct), 09.00–18.00 Tues–Sun, closed Mon (Nov–Mar) ⓝ Bus: 8 to Musée Olympique. Admission charge

Opéra de Lausanne (Lausanne Opera)

The acclaimed Lausanne Opera presents an eclectic repertoire of opera, dance, classical concerts and recitals. The season runs from September to May.

ⓐ 12 Avenue du Théâtre ⓣ 021 310 16 00

ⓦ www.opera-lausanne.ch ⓔ opera@lausanne.ch

ⓛ 09.00–18.30 Mon–Sun ⓝ Bus: 9, 12 to Georgette

Palais de Rumine (Rumine Palace)

The sheer scale of this neo-Renaissance building towering above Place de la Riponne is impressive. The ornate façade shelters a clutch of fascinating museums, including the Fine Arts Museum, the Archaeology and History Museum, and the Zoological Museum. Highlights include the reconstruction of a Neolithic cave and masterpieces by Swiss artist Charles Gleyre.
ⓐ Place de la Riponne ⓣ 021 692 44 70 ⓛ 11.00–18.00 Tues–Thur, 11.00–17.00 Fri–Sun, closed Mon ⓝ Bus: 5, 6, 8 to Riponne. Admission charge

▲ The magnificent Palais de Rumine

RETAIL THERAPY

Art Suisse Contemporary creations by Swiss artists are the big draw here. ⓐ 8 Rue Enning ⓣ 021 320 81 80 ⓛ 12.30–18.15 Tues–Fri, 09.30–17.00 Sat, closed Sun ⓝ Bus: 17 to Benjamin-Constant

Durig Cocoa-mad Dan Durig creates divine sweets including Venezuelan milk truffles and organic chocolate plums. ⓐ 15 Avenue d'Ouchy ⓣ 021 601 24 35 ⓦ www.durig.ch ⓛ 08.30–18.30 Tues–Fri, 08.30–17.00 Sat, closed Sun & Mon ⓝ Bus: 2 to Closelet

La Ferme Vaudoise Near the town hall, this store is well stocked with Vaud specialities, from Mont d'Or cheese to handmade sausages. ⓐ 5 Place de la Palud ⓣ 021 351 35 55 ⓛ 09.00–13.00, 14.00–18.30 Mon–Fri, 07.30–17.00 Sat, closed Sun ⓝ Bus: 16 to Pierre-Viret

L'Herboriste This old-world shop is crammed with herbal teas, remedies, natural cosmetics, fragrances and essential oils. ⓐ 12 Avenue du Léman ⓣ 021 311 81 70 ⓦ www.lherboriste.ch ⓛ 14.00–19.00 Mon, 14.30–19.00 Tues–Fri, 09.00–17.00 Sat, closed Sun ⓝ Bus: 9 to Avenue du Léman

TheTeaTee Around 160 blends of tea and delicate china line the walls of this inviting shop. Look out for the exclusive Me Tseng vintage. ⓐ 4 Rue Enning ⓣ 021 312 48 63 ⓦ www.theteatee.ch ⓛ 13.30–18.30 Mon, 09.30–18.30 Tues–Fri, 09.30–17.00 Sat, closed Sun ⓝ Bus: 17 to Benjamin-Constant

TAKING A BREAK

Délices du Chocolat £ The sweet-toothed should make for this smart tearoom for luscious apple tarts, petits fours and pastries. Pick up some cocoa-dusted truffles on your way out. ⓐ 2–4 Rue Enning ⓣ 02 320 24 24 ⓛ 07.00–19.00 Mon–Fri, 07.00–18.00 Sat, 07.00–13.00 Sun ⓝ Bus: 17 to Benjamin-Constant

L'Éléphant Blanc £ In the heart of the Old Town, this charming restaurant's menu is limited but superbly cooked, from duck foie gras to crème brulée. ⓐ 4 Rue Cité-Devant ⓣ 021 312 71 77 ⓛ 11.00–24.00 Mon–Fri, closed Sat & Sun ⓝ Bus: 16 to Pierre-Viret

🔺 *Specially for the sweet-toothed: Délices du Chocolat*

Fox Café £ This spacious New York-style diner serves up tasty omelettes, curries, pasta dishes and mussels. ⓐ 10 Rue Enning ① 021 323 32 18 ● 07.30–01.00 Mon–Thur, 07.30–02.00 Fri & Sat, 17.00–01.00 Sun ⓝ Bus: 17 to Benjamin-Constant

AFTER DARK

Restaurants

Au Couscous £ Glammed up with oriental mosaics, this hole-in-the-wall restaurant is a well-kept secret. Savour Lebanese mezze, merguez and sticky baklava. ⓐ 2 Rue Enning ① 021 321 38 48 ⓦ www.au-couscous.ch ● 11.30–14.30, 18.30–01.00 Mon–Sat, 18.30–24.00 Sun ⓝ Bus: 17 to Benjamin-Constant

Café Romand £ Enjoy cheese fondue at this elegant Swiss brasserie, which has high ceilings, moody lighting and wood panelling. ⓐ 2 Place Saint-François ① 021 312 63 75 ⓦ www.caferomand.com ● 09.00–01.00 Mon–Sat, closed Sun ⓝ Bus: 2, 4, 8 to St-François

Le Java £ This galleried restaurant fuses arabesque touches with art deco nostalgia. The menu is equally inspired. ⓐ 26 Rue Marterey ① 021 321 38 37 ⓦ www.lejava.ch ● 08.00–24.00 Mon–Fri, 08.00–02.00 Sat & Sun ⓝ Bus: 17 to Benjamin-Constant

À la Pomme de Pin ££ Tucked down a street near the cathedral, this brasserie serves classic specialities. ⓐ 11–13 Rue Cité-Derrière ① 021 323 46 56 ● 08.00–24.00 Mon–Fri, 18.00–24.00 Sat, closed Sun ⓝ Bus: 16 to Pierre-Viret

Bars & clubs

Bleu Lezard One of Lausanne's hippest haunts, this upbeat bar draws a lively crowd.  10 Rue Enning  021 323 00 55  www.bleulezard.ch  07.00–01.00 Mon–Thur, 07.00–02.00 Fri, 08.00–02.00 Sat, 09.30–01.00 Sun  Bus: 17 to Benjamin-Constant

Les Brasseurs Copper vats and wood floors make this micro-brewery an inviting place to enjoy a beer and sauerkraut.  4 Rue Centrale  021 351 14 24  www.les-brasseurs.ch  11.00–01.00 Mon–Thur, 11.00–02.00 Fri & Sat, 16.00–24.00 Sun  Bus: 2 to Bel-Air

Captain Cook Pub This cheery English pub serves real ales and bar food and shows big-screen sports.  2 Rue Enning  021 323 00 55  www.captain-cook.ch  08.30–01.00 Mon–Thur, 08.30–02.00 Fri, 14.00–02.00 Sat, 16.00–01.00 Sun  Bus: 17 to Benjamin-Constant

D'Club Party till dawn to live acts and electro-house music at this funky club.  15 Place Centrale  021 351 51 40  www.dclub.ch  21.00–02.00 Wed, 21.00–04.00 Thur, 21.00–05.00 Fri & Sat, closed Sun & Mon  Bus: 2 to Bel-Air

Le Lounge Part of Ouchy's medieval château, this lounge-style bar affords uninterrupted views of the lake through floor-to-ceiling glass windows.  2 Place du Port  021 616 74 51  www.chateaudouchy.ch  09.00–01.00 Mon–Thur, 09.00–02.00 Fri & Sat, 16.00–24.00 Sun  Bus: 2 to Ouchy

ACCOMMODATION

Camping Vidy £ A stone's throw from Ouchy, this lakefront campsite has a supermarket, play area, laundry and restaurant. ⓐ 3 Chemin du Camping ⓣ 021 622 50 00 ⓦ www.campinglausannevidy.ch ⓔ info@clv.ch ⓛ Apr–Oct, closed Nov–Mar ⓝ Bus: 2 to Bois de Vaux

Lausanne YH £ Set in attractive grounds by the lake, this hostel features clean and bright singles, doubles and dorms. ⓐ 36 Chemin du Bois-du-Vaux ⓣ 021 626 02 22 ⓦ www.youthhostel.ch ⓔ lausanne@youthhostel.ch ⓝ Bus: 2 to Bois de Vaux

Hôtel Élite ££ Surrounded by gardens, this recently renovated hotel is one of Lausanne's best mid-range options. Choose the top floor for lake views. ⓐ 1 Avenue Sainte-Luce ⓣ 021 320 23 61 ⓦ www.elite-lausanne.ch ⓔ info@elite-lausanne.ch ⓝ Bus: 2, 4, 8 to St-François

VINE TIME

At the heart of vine-clad Vaud, the precipitous terraces surrounding Lausanne are prime wine-growing territory. A great way to explore them is to don walking boots or hire a bicycle, pausing in the cellars en route. The 33-km (20-mile) stretch from Ouchy to Chillon passes through villages like Lutry, Riex and Chardonne and will give you intoxicating alpine views.

Annecy

Situated on the northern tip of turquoise Lake Annecy, it's easy to see Annecy's appeal: pure alpine waters framed by jagged peaks, flower-lined canals and a medieval castle overshadowing the Old Town's warren of cobbled streets. Life here is laid-back, and simple pleasures like savouring fresh lake trout or strolling on waterfront promenades are a delight. For those seeking more adventure, Annecy's big and beautiful backyard provides a range of outdoor action including kayaking, climbing and skiing in the nearby Alps.

● *The turquoise tranquillity of Lake Annecy*

GETTING THERE

The speedy A41 motorway links Geneva to Annecy in just 40 minutes. The French town is also accessible by public transport, with SNCF trains operating a frequent service to Annecy's main station. Sibra buses serve the town and surrounding villages. Ⓦ www.sibra.fr

SIGHTS & ATTRACTIONS

Basilique de la Visitation

On top of a wooded hill, this early 20th-century basilica features a striking 72-m (236-ft) steeple and offers sweeping views over Annecy.

ⓐ 20 Avenue de la Visitation ⓣ 04 50 45 22 76
ⓔ musees@anglo-annecy.fr ⓛ 07.00–12.00, 14.00–19.00 Mon–Sun Ⓝ Bus: 14 to Visitation

Château d'Annecy (Annecy Castle)

Set against a backdrop of snow-capped mountains, this red-turreted castle looms large above Annecy. Sturdy towers soar above the cobbled inner courtyard, the oldest dating back to the 13th century. From this fairy-tale perch, you can enjoy superb views of the lake and town.

ⓐ Place du Château ⓣ 04 50 33 87 30
ⓔ musees@anglo-annecy.fr ⓛ 10.00–12.00, 14.00–17.00 Wed–Mon, closed Tues (Oct–May); 10.30–18.00 Mon–Sun (June–Sept) Ⓝ Bus: 7, 14 to Paradis

Jardins de l'Europe

Locals hang out by the lake's edge in these pristine gardens, which have plenty of shady nooks in which to relax and watch the world go by. Enjoy a picnic beneath the shady trees, stroll to Lovers' Bridge and glimpse the tiny Île des Cygnes (Swan Island).

ⓐ Quai Napoleon III ⓥ Bus: 6, 7, 15 to Hôtel de Ville

🔺 *From town gaol to tourist delight: Palais de l'Île*

Palais de l'Île

Annecy's picture-perfect landmark belies its function as the town's former prison. With its wistful turrets rising high above the Thiou Canal, this medieval icon is one of France's most photographed buildings. Step inside to explore a labyrinth of cells and wander the banks to watch local artists at work. After dark, the illuminated prison is enchanting.

🅐 3 Passage de l'Île ☎ 04 50 33 87 30 ✉ musees@anglo-annecy.fr 🕐 10.00–12.00, 14.00–17.00 Wed–Mon, closed Tues (Oct–May); 10.30–18.00 Mon–Sun (June–Sept) 🚌 Bus: 6, 7, 15 to Hôtel de Ville. Admission charge

Pont des Amours (Lovers' Bridge)

Straddling the Vassé Canal, this arched bridge links the Jardins de l'Europe to Champs de Mars promenade. Romantic couples come here to walk hand in hand; singletons can fall in love with the views of Lake Annecy instead.

🅐 Champs de Mars 🕐 Bus: 6, 7, 15 to Hôtel de Ville

CULTURE

Musée Château d'Annecy (Annecy Castle Museum)

Housed in the castle, this museum traces Annecy's intriguing history, with its displays of traditional Savoy furniture, contemporary art and alpine anthropology.

🅐 Place du Château ☎ 04 50 33 87 30 ✉ musees@anglo-annecy.fr 🕐 10.00–12.00, 14.00–17.00 Wed–Mon, closed Tues (Oct–May); 10.30–18.00 Mon–Sun (June–Sept) 🚌 Bus: 7, 14 to Paradis. Admission charge

RECREATION

Bateaux Dupraz A mini-cruise is a relaxed way to tour the glistening lake and see the sights from the water. Boats with guided commentary depart regularly in summer.
ⓐ Jardins de l'Europe ⓣ 04 50 52 42 99
ⓦ www.bateauxdupraz.com ⓛ 11.00, 14.15, 15.00, 16.15, 17.15
Mon–Sun ⓝ Bus: 6, 7, 15 to Hôtel de Ville

Gorges du Fier A 15-minute journey from Annecy, Lovagny boasts one of France's most dramatic river gorges. This precipitous ravine's bizarre rock formations and high footbridges are very impressive.
ⓐ Lovagny ⓣ 04 50 46 23 07 ⓦ www.gorgesdufier.com
ⓛ 09.15–18.00 Mon–Sun (Mar–Oct); closed Nov–Feb ⓝ Bus: 62 to Lovagny. Admission charge

LocaLoisirs This centre in nearby Annecy-le-Vieux rents kayaks, mountain bikes and scooters, as well as organising activities like paragliding, rafting and canoeing. ⓐ 47 Avenue du Petit Port

KING OF 12 CASTLES...
Passing through Annecy, the Road of the Dukes of Savoy links 12 historic castles, abbeys and forts. As well as tracing the region's fascinating heritage, the route takes in some spectacular alpine scenery.
ⓦ www.chateaux-france.com/route-savoie

From pedaloes to paragliding, Annecy provides a range of diversions

🕿 04 50 23 31 15 ⓦ www.annecy-loca-loisirs.com 🕓 09.00–19.00 Mon–Sun (Apr–Oct); closed Nov–Mar 🔄 Bus: 15 to Annecy-le-Vieux/Pré Vernet

Marquisats Swimming Pool and Beach With its trio of outdoor pools, this lido by the lake is the ideal spot to swim and relax in summer. 🅰 29 Rue des Marquisats 🕿 04 50 33 65 40 🕓 09.00–19.30 Mon–Fri, 09.00–19.00 Sat, 10.00–19.00 Sun (May–Sept); closed Oct–Apr 🔄 Bus: 6, 7, 14 to Hôpital Marquisats. Admission charge

Takamaka Adrenaline junkies get their thrills with activities like canyoning, sky diving, downhill mountain biking and paragliding at this extreme sports centre. 🅰 23 Faubourg Sainte-Claire 🕿 04 50 45 60 61 ⓦ www.takamaka.fr 📧 info@takamaka.fr 🕓 09.00–19.00 Mon–Sun (Apr–Oct); closed Nov–Mar 🔄 Bus: 4, 7 to Fauré

RETAIL THERAPY

Courier This modern shopping mall shelters 40 high-street stores under its glass roof, including names like H&M, Fnac and Sephora. 🅰 65 Rue Carnot 🕿 04 50 46 46 76 ⓦ www.centre-courier.com 🕓 09.30–19.30 Mon–Sat, closed Sun 🔄 Bus: 2, 6, 10 to Courier

Crèmerie du Lac Cheese Fans of *fromage* sniff Alain Michel's store, crammed with different cheeses. Look out for Savoy classics like flavoursome Reblochon and Roquefort ripened in a cool cellar.

ⓐ 3 Rue du Lac ⓣ 04 50 45 19 31 ⓦ www.cremeriedulac.com
ⓛ 09.30–19.30 Mon–Sat; closed Sun ⓝ Bus: 6, 7, 15 to Hôtel
de Ville

Farmers' Market Potter around Annecy's vibrant market, where
stalls are piled high with local produce, from wheels of Savoy
cheese to fresh fruit, plump olives, sausages and handmade
bread. ⓐ Rue de la République, Rue Sainte-Claire, Pont-Morens
ⓛ 08.00–12.00 Tues, Fri & Sun ⓝ Bus: 6, 7, 15 to Hôtel de Ville

TAKING A BREAK

Au Fidèle Berger £ It's hard to resist *les cloches d'Annecy* (bells of
Annecy) pralines here, where the scent of hot chocolate fills the
air. If you're sweet enough already, try one of the speciality teas.
ⓐ 2 Rue Royale ⓣ 04 50 45 00 32 ⓛ 08.45–19.00 Tues–Sat, closed
Sun & Mon ⓝ Bus: 6, 7, 15 to Hôtel de Ville

Nature et Saveur £ The freshest local produce is used to create
vegetarian options, fresh salads and healthy (!) desserts.
ⓐ Place des Cordeliers ⓣ 04 50 45 82 29
ⓦ www.nature-saveur.com ⓛ 08.30–19.00 Tues–Sat, closed Sun
& Mon ⓝ Bus: 6, 7, 15 to Hôtel de Ville

Passion Gourmande £ If you're crazy about crêpes, this
central café is for you. The lunch menu offers great value and
there is a sunny terrace. ⓐ 16 Rue Sainte-Claire ⓣ 04 50 52 92 78
ⓛ 12.00–14.00, 19.00–23.00 Mon–Sun ⓝ Bus: 6, 7, 15 to Hôtel
de Ville

AFTER DARK

Restaurants

Le Lilas Rose £ When it's cold outside, this canal-side bistro dishes up hearty alpine fare like raclette, gooey fondue and tartiflettes. **ⓐ** Passage de l'Évêché **ⓣ** 04 50 45 37 08 **ⓛ** 12.00–14.00, 19.00–23.00 Mon–Sun **ⓝ** Bus: 6, 7, 15 to Hôtel de Ville

Le Munich £ This lively brasserie and bar overlooks the Thiou Canal. Munch on sauerkraut with sausage, knuckle of ham or mussels and chips. There are 13 draught beers to choose from. **ⓐ** 1 Quai Perrière **ⓣ** 04 50 45 02 11 **ⓦ** www.lemunich.com **ⓛ** 08.00–02.00 Mon–Sun **ⓝ** Bus: 6, 7, 15 to Hôtel de Ville

Super Panorama £ The name of this restaurant says it all: the lake and mountain views from the terrace are as appetising as the cuisine. Try the trout with almonds with a glass of crisp Apremont. **ⓐ** 7 Route du Semnoz **ⓣ** 04 50 45 34 86 **ⓦ** www.super-panorama.com **ⓛ** 12.00–16.00 Mon, 12.00–22.00 Wed–Sun, closed Tues **ⓝ** Bus: 6 to Hôtel de Police

Auberge de Savoie ££ Fish doesn't come fresher than at this gourmet haunt, located on an attractive square opposite the Palais de l'Île. **ⓐ** 1 Place Saint François de Sales **ⓣ** 04 50 45 03 05 **ⓦ** www.aubergedesavoie.fr **ⓛ** 11.30–15.00, 19.00–23.00 Thur–Mon, closed Tues & Wed **ⓝ** Bus: 6, 7, 15 to Hôtel de Ville

La Ciboulette ££–£££ Georges Paccard cooks up a storm at this gem of a restaurant. Specialities include Pauillac lamb and filet of turbot, all served on the terrace. ⓐ 10 Rue Vaugelas ⓣ 04 50 45 74 57 ⓛ 12.00–14.00, 19.00–23.00 Tues–Sat, closed Sun & Mon ⓝ Bus: 6, 7, 15 to Hôtel de Ville

Bars & clubs

Finn Kelly's A favourite among Annecy's students, this relaxed Irish pub has regular jam sessions, free wireless internet, big-screen sports and a terrace where you can sip Beamish Stout. ⓐ 10 Faubourg Annonciades ⓣ 04 50 51 29 40 ⓦ www.finnkellys.com ⓝ Bus: 6, 7, 15 to Hôtel de Ville

Red'z Partygoers head for this hip club in the heart of Annecy, where DJs spin techno and house. ⓐ 4 Quai Perrière ⓣ 04 50 45 02 11 ⓦ www.red-z.net ⓛ 11.00–03.00 Mon–Sun (Apr–Sept); 15.30–03.00 Mon–Sun (Oct–Mar) ⓝ Bus: 6, 7, 15 to Hôtel de Ville

ACCOMMODATION

Annecy AJ £ A brisk uphill hike takes you to this cheery lodge-style hostel, bordering the forest and affording superb views. It has a snug bar, spotless dorms and provides good-value meals. ⓐ 4 Route du Semnoz ⓣ 04 50 45 33 19 ⓦ http://auberge-annecy.com ⓔ annecy@fuaj.org ⓛ Apr–Oct; closed Nov–Mar ⓝ Bus: 6 to Hôtel de Police

Camping Le Belvédère £ This is close enough to the lake for a dip before breakfast, only 10 minutes from the beach and the Old

Town. On-site facilities at this green and tranquil location include a laundry, mini-market and playground. ⓐ 8 Route du Semnoz ⓣ 04 50 45 48 30 ⓕ 04 50 51 81 62 ⓔ camping@ville-annecy.fr ⓛ Apr–Oct; closed Nov–Mar ⓝ Bus: 6 to Hôtel de Police

Hôtel du Château £ Nestled at the foot of the castle, this family-run hotel has an intimate feel. Rooms are simple but comfortable and offer fine views. ⓐ 16 Rampe du Château ⓣ 04 50 45 27 66 ⓕ 04 50 52 75 26 ⓦ www.annecy-hotel.com ⓔ hotelduchateau@noos.fr ⓝ Bus: 7, 14 to Paradis

Hôtel du Nord £ Close to the lake, this peaceful hotel is an ideal base. The rooms are decorated in warm hues and feature modern bathrooms. There is free parking and a generous breakfast buffet. ⓐ 24 Rue Sommeiller ⓣ 04 50 45 08 78 ⓕ 04 50 51 22 04 ⓦ www.annecy-hotel-du-nord.com ⓔ contact@annecy-hotel-du-nord.com ⓝ Bus: 6, 7, 15 to Hôtel de Ville

● *Geneva's riverside tourist office*

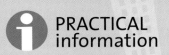

PRACTICAL
information

Directory

GETTING THERE

By air

Many airlines operate a frequent, direct service between Genèva-Cointrin International Airport (GVA) and around 90 destinations such as London, New York and Rome. Among them are budget airlines such as bmibaby and easyJet, as well as British Airways and American Airlines. Just eight minutes from the centre, Geneva's ultra-modern airport offers excellent facilities including shops, ATMs and a post office.

American Airlines Ⓦ www.aa.com

bmibaby Ⓦ www.bmibaby.com

British Airways Ⓦ www.britishairways.com

easyJet Ⓦ www.easyjet.com

Swiss Ⓦ www.swiss.com

Many people are aware that air travel emits CO_2, which contributes to climate change. You may be interested in the possibility of lessening the environmental impact of your flight through the charity Climate Care, which offsets your CO_2 by funding environmental projects around the world. Visit Ⓦ www.climatecare.org

By bus

International and long-distance buses depart from Geneva's main bus station on Place Dorcière, operating to destinations including Lyon, Rome and London.

City Bus Ⓦ www.citybus.ch

Eurolines Ⓦ www.eurolines.com

By car

Switzerland's roads are well maintained, driving is on the right and international signs are used. The speed limit is strictly enforced, with cameras operating on most stretches of motorways and speeding offences often subject to hefty on-the-spot fines. To drive on Switzerland's motorways, you'll need to purchase a *Vignette* (toll sticker) to display in the front windscreen. On a clear run, you can reach Lausanne in 45 minutes, Lyon in 1 hour 30 minutes and Zurich in 2 hours 30 minutes.

By rail

Geneva's main station, Gare Cornavin, has excellent connections on high-speed trains to major Swiss cities including Lausanne, Bern, Basel and Zurich, as well as serving European cities including Lyon, Paris, Barcelona and Venice. Swiss Federal Railways provides detailed information on routes and timetables.

SBB Ⓦ www.sbb.ch

🔺 *Gare Cornavin, the central railway station*

ENTRY FORMALITIES
Documentation
EU, Australian, Canadian, New Zealand, South African and United States citizens must have a valid passport to enter Switzerland, but do not require a visa for stays of fewer than 90 days. If you are arriving from countries other than these, you may need a visa and should contact your consulate or embassy up to three months before departure. The Swiss Federal Department of Foreign Affairs provides more information on entry requirements at ⓦ www.eda.admin.ch

Customs
It is usually free to import goods from a non-EU country, but you should check restrictions on the imports of tobacco, perfume and alcohol. Further information is available at ⓦ www.ezv.admin.ch

MONEY
Switzerland's currency is the Swiss franc (CHF), divided up into 100 rappen or centimes. One Swiss franc is roughly the equivalent of £0.40, $0.80 or €0.60. Coins are in denominations of CHF5, 2 and 1, and 50, 20, 10 and 5 centimes. There are banknotes of 10, 20, 50, 100, 200, 500 and 1,000 francs. Many of Geneva's restaurants, hotels and shops also accept euros.

Central Geneva has plenty of ATMs where you can withdraw cash with your credit card 24 hours a day, although it's worth checking whether the bank imposes a fee. Most banks open 08.30–16.30 Monday to Friday.

There are bureaux de change in banks, the main train station and the airport. Traveller's cheques can be cashed in most bureaux de change, banks, travel agencies and hotels. Banks generally offer the best rates. Visa, MasterCard, Diners Club and American Express are widely accepted.

HEALTH, SAFETY & CRIME

Geneva is a clean and safe city to visit, and there are no particular health risks. No immunisations or health certificates are required and the tap water is safe to drink.

While Switzerland has one of the best standards of medical care in the world, treatment can be expensive, so it's wise to invest in a good health insurance policy before visiting. EU citizens are entitled to free or reduced-cost emergency health care with a valid European Health Insurance Card (EHIC), which entitles you to state medical treatment but does not cover repatriation or long-term illness.

Pharmacies can treat minor ailments and are usually open 07.45–18.30 Monday to Friday and 08.00–17.00 Saturday. The Geneva Pharmacies Association lists 24-hour pharmacies at ⓦ www.pharmacies-geneve.ch. Your hotel should be able to arrange for you to see an English-speaking doctor, if necessary.

The crime rate in Geneva is low, so you shouldn't experience any problems during your stay. However, pickpockets may operate in key tourist areas, so it's wise to keep an eye on your possessions. If you are the victim of a crime, you should inform the police by calling 117 (see *Emergencies*, page 138).

OPENING HOURS
Banks
Banks open 08.00–16.30 Monday to Friday. All close at weekends, but many have 24-hour ATMs.

Shops
Most shops open 09.00–19.00 Monday to Saturday; smaller boutiques often close for lunch. Shopping malls and department stores stay open until 21.00 on Thursdays.

TOILETS
There are clean public toilets in the centre of Geneva, with most offering baby-changing facilities and access to disabled travellers. You'll need 50 centimes to use the city's automatic, self-cleaning toilets. Most cafés, restaurants and some department stores have free toilets for customers.

CHILDREN
Extremely clean and easy to negotiate, this family-friendly city has a range of attractions to keep children amused. There is usually a 50 per cent reduction for children, and kids are welcome in most restaurants and cafés.

Bains des Pâquis The Right Bank's pier is a relaxed spot for families to enjoy a picnic and swim (see page 76).

Bois de la Bâtie (Bâtie Woods) Children will love to explore the caves, gorges and woodlands. There's also a splash pool and playground. ⓐ Bâtie ⓝ Bus: 2, 10, 11 to Bâtie

Geneva Card Families can save by purchasing a Geneva Card, offering free access to the public transport network and entry to many top museums and attractions, plus reductions in some shops and restaurants. The card is available for 24 or 72 hours.

Genève-Plage (Geneva Beach) Tots enjoy the paddling pool, sandpit and slides here, while teens head for the Olympic Swimming Pool, diving boards and volleyball court (see page 35).

◗ There's plenty of fun for kids

Mini-train In summer, a mini-train chugs through Geneva's streets to take in the key sights. ⓐ Rotonde du Mont-Blanc ⓣ 022 781 04 04 ⓦ www.sttr.ch ⓛ 10.00–dusk Mon–Sun (Mar–Oct) ⓝ Bus: 8 to Chantepoulet

Vivarium Lausanne Children can spot crocodiles, turtles, anacondas and lizards at one of Europe's leading vivariums. ⓐ 82 Chemin de Boissonnet, Lausanne ⓣ 021 652 72 94 ⓦ www.vivarium-lausanne.ch ⓔ info@vivarium-lausanne.ch ⓛ 14.00–17.30 Mon–Fri, 10.00–17.30 Sat & Sun ⓝ Bus: 14 to Mont. Admission charge

COMMUNICATIONS
Phones
Geneva's modern public telephone boxes are simple to use and rates reasonable. Only some phones accept coins, so you'll

DIALLING CODES
Telephoning Geneva
Dial 00 41 for Switzerland, then 22 for Geneva followed by the seven-digit number.

Telephoning abroad
To call out of Switzerland, simply dial 00 followed by the country code and the local number.

Directory Enquiries ⓣ 1811
International Operator ⓣ 1141

probably need to buy a prepaid phone card or use your credit card (no surcharge). The GSM 900/1800 mobile phone networks operate in Switzerland.

Post
You can purchase stamps in post offices and some newsagents. The main post office in the city centre is on Rue du Mont-Blanc. Ⓦ www.swisspost.ch

Internet
There are a handful of internet cafés in the centre of Geneva that offer a high-speed broadband connection. Expect to pay between CHF5 and CHF10 for an hour online.

Charly's Check Point Open 24 hours, this offers internet access as well as services like scanning and faxing. ⓐ 7 Rue de Fribourg ⓣ 022 901 13 13 Ⓦ www.charlys.com Ⓛ 09.00–24.00 Mon–Sat, 14.00–22.00 Sun Ⓝ Tram: 13, 15 to Cornavin

Cyber-Café 3000 This cheery café has a reliable internet connection, plus printers and scanners. ⓐ 2 Rue Henri-Christine ⓣ 022 320 74 55 Ⓛ 11.00–21.00 Mon–Sun Ⓝ Tram: 13 to Pont-d'Arve

Las Vegas Mont-Blanc Cyberland Conveniently located near the main station. ⓐ 26 Rue du Mont-Blanc ⓣ 022 738 57 44 Ⓝ Tram: 13, 15 to Cornavin

Laundrenet Doubling as a laundrette, this place offers a high-speed internet connection, scanner and colour printing.

ⓐ 83 Rue de la Servette ⓣ 022 733 83 83 ⓦ www.laundrenet.ch
ⓛ 12.00–22.00 Mon & Wed, 09.00–22.00 Tues & Thur,
09.00–21.00 Fri & Sat, 12.00–20.00 Sun ⓝ Bus: 9 to Poterie

Wi-fi hotspots

Wireless internet access (wi-fi) has become widespread in
Geneva with many cafés, restaurants, bars, hotels and even
petrol stations offering the service. The following website
gives details on free hotspots in Switzerland
ⓦ www.freespots.ch.

ELECTRICITY

Switzerland's electricity system is very reliable. It is 220 volts,
50 hertz (round, three-pin plugs). Adaptors and transformers are
available for visitors.

TRAVELLERS WITH DISABILITIES

Geneva caters to travellers with special needs. Most of the city's
key attractions are accessible for visitors with disabilities,
including MAMCO, the Palace of Nations and the International
Red Cross Museum; many offer concessions (*tarif réduit*) or free
entry. If notified in advance, Swiss Federal Railways (SBB) can
assist wheelchair users and passengers with reduced mobility.
ⓣ 0800 007 102

Switzerland Mobility International Switzerland (MIS)
ⓐ 4 Froburgstrasse, Olten ⓣ 062 206 88 35 ⓦ www.mis-ch.ch
ⓔ info@mis-ch.ch

UK & Ireland British Council of Disabled People (BCDP)
ⓣ 01332 295551 ⓦ www.bcodp.org.uk ⓔ general@bcodp.org.uk

US & Canada Society for Accessible Travel & Hospitality (SATH)
ⓐ 347 Fifth Ave, New York ⓣ 212 447 7284 ⓦ www.sath.org;
Access-Able ⓦ www.access-able.com
Australia & New Zealand Accessibility
ⓦ www.accessibility.com.au; Disabled Persons Assembly
ⓣ 04 801 9100 ⓦ www.dpa.org.nz

FURTHER INFORMATION

Geneva Tourism
ⓐ 18 Rue du Mont-Blanc ⓣ 022 909 70 00 ⓕ 022 909 70 11
ⓦ www.geneve-tourisme.ch ⓔ info@geneve-tourisme.ch
ⓛ 10.00–18.00 Mon, 09.00–18.00 Tues–Sat, closed Sun (winter);
10.00–18.00 Mon, 09.00–18.00 Tues–Sun (summer)

Lausanne Tourism ⓐ 9 Place de la Gare ⓣ 021 613 73 73 ⓕ 021 616
86 47 ⓦ www.lausanne-tourisme.ch ⓔ information@lausanne-
tourisme.ch ⓛ 09.00–19.00 Mon–Sun

Annecy Tourist Office ⓐ 1 Rue Jean-Jaurès ⓣ 04 50 45 00 33 ⓕ 04
50 51 87 20 ⓦ www.lac-annecy.com ⓔ info@annecytourisme.
com ⓛ 09.00–12.00, 13.45–18.00 Mon–Sat

Carouge Tourist Information ⓦ www.carouge.ch

Emergencies

EMERGENCY NUMBERS

The following are national free emergency numbers:

Police 🛈 117
Fire 🛈 118
Ambulance 🛈 144
Emergency 🛈 112
Breakdown 🛈 140
On-call doctors 🛈 022 748 49 50

When you dial the Europe-wide emergency number 112, ask for the service you require and give details of where you are, what the emergency is and the number of the phone you are using. The operator will connect you to the service you need.

Open 24 hours a day, seven days a week, the police station at Gare Cornavin can be reached by calling 🛈 022 388 61 00.

MEDICAL SERVICES

It is strongly recommended to have a valid health insurance policy before travelling to Switzerland. EU citizens are entitled to free or reduced-cost emergency health care with a European Health Insurance Card (EHIC). Pharmacies usually open 07.45–18.30 Monday to Friday and 08.00–17.00 Saturday, but some stay open 24 hours. For details on late-opening pharmacies, call 🛈 022 306 08 50

The centrally located Geneva University Hospital (HUG) provides emergency treatment. 🅰 24 Rue Micheli-du-Crest 🛈 022 372 33 11 🅦 www.hug-ge.ch

CONSULATES

Australia ⓐ 2 Chemin des Fins ⓣ 022 799 91 00 ⓕ 022 799 91 78
ⓦ www.australia.ch ⓛ 09.00–17.00 Mon–Fri, closed Sat & Sun
UK ⓐ 37–39 Rue de Vermont ⓣ 022 918 24 18 ⓕ 022 918 23 22
ⓦ www.britishembassy.gov.uk ⓛ 08.30–12.30, 14.00–17.00
Mon–Fri, closed Sat & Sun

EMBASSIES

Canada ⓐ 88 Kirchenfeldstrasse, Bern ⓣ 031 357 32 00
ⓦ www.bern.gc.ca ⓛ 08.00–12.00, 13.00–17.00 Mon–Thur,
08.00–13.30 Fri
Ireland ⓐ 68 Kirchenfeldstrasse, Bern ⓣ 031 352 14 42
ⓕ 031 352 14 55 ⓔ berneembassy@dfa.ie
South Africa ⓐ 29 Alpenstrasse, Bern ⓣ 031 350 13 13
ⓦ www.southafrica.ch ⓛ 08.00–12.30, 13.30–17.15 Mon–Thur,
08.00–12.00, 13.00–15.00 Fri
UK ⓐ 50 Thunstrasse, Bern ⓣ 031 359 77 00 ⓦ www.britain-in-
switzerland.ch ⓛ 09.00–13.00, 14.00–17.00 Mon–Fri
USA ⓐ 95 Jubilaumsstrasse, Bern ⓣ 031 357 72 34
ⓦ http://bern.usembassy.gov ⓛ 09.00–11.30 Mon–Fri

EMERGENCY PHRASES
Help! Au secours! *Ossercoor!*　**Fire!** Au feu! *Oh fur!*
Stop! Stop! *Stop!*
Call an ambulance/a doctor/the police/the fire service!
Appelez une ambulance/un médecin/la police/les pompiers!
*Ahperleh ewn ahngbewlahngss/ang medesang/lah poleess/
leh pompeeyeh!*

The publishers would like to thank the following individuals and organisations for providing their copyright photographs for this book:
Andy Christiani pages 3, 7, 9, 17, 18, 34, 42, 65, 77, 81, 92, 94, 105, 110; Manotel page 39; Pictures Colour Library pages 45, 121; World Pictures/Photoshot pages 103, 116, 118; all the rest Jonathan Smith

Copy editor: Penny Isaac
Proofreader: Ian Faulkner

Send your thoughts to
books@thomascook.com

- **Found a great bar, club, shop or must-see sight that we don't feature?**

- **Like to tip us off about any information that needs updating?**

- **Want to tell us what you love about this handy little guidebook and more importantly how we can make it even handier?**

Then here's your chance to tell all! Send us ideas, discoveries and recommendations today and then look out for your valuable input in the next edition of this title. As an extra 'thank you' from Thomas Cook Publishing, you'll be automatically entered into our exciting prize draw.

Send an email to the above address (stating the book's title) or write to:
CitySpots Project Editor, Thomas Cook Publishing, PO Box 227, The Thomas Cook Business Park, Unit 18, Coningsby Road, Peterborough PE3 8SB, UK.